Russian Public Diplomacy

Public diplomacy is widely used in the contemporary world, and this book is devoted to its use and study in Russia.

It explores how, even though scientific diplomacy and people's diplomacy were used in the USSR, the ideas of public diplomacy were not in demand in Russia in the 1990s. However, following the United States, which turned to the policy after the tragic events of 9/11, Russia also began to develop its own. The author explores how the need for public diplomacy is reflected in the official documents of the Russian Federation and discusses the important step of building new institutions for this purpose in Russia. She analyzes how the development of the practice has led to its study, with Russian scholars focusing mainly on the tools and approaches of implementing public diplomacy by various states. The book discusses the relationship between public diplomacy and soft power and compares Russian approaches with those available in worldwide practice and theory.

This book is intended primarily for students and researchers of international affairs specializing in Russian foreign policy and/or soft power issues. It will also be of interest to practitioners in public diplomacy, such as ministers of foreign affairs, NGOs, and the media.

Marina M. Lebedeva is Professor and Head of the World Politics Department at Moscow State Institute of International Relations (MGIMO-University), Russia. Her research interests include world politics; conflict management, negotiations, and public diplomacy; and education in the field of IR.

Innovations in International Affairs
Series Editor: Raffaele Marchetti
LUISS Guido Carli, Italy

Innovations in International Affairs aims to provide cutting-edge analyses of controversial trends in international affairs with the intent to innovate our understanding of global politics. Hosting mainstream as well as alternative stances, the series promotes both the re-assessment of traditional topics and the exploration of new aspects.

The series invites both engaged scholars and reflective practitioners, and is committed to bringing non-western voices into current debates.

Innovations in International Affairs is keen to consider new book proposals in the following key areas:

- **Innovative topics**: related to aspects that have remained marginal in scholarly and public debates
- **International crises**: related to the most urgent contemporary phenomena and how to interpret and tackle them
- **World perspectives**: related mostly to non-western points of view

Titles in this series include:

Trump and the Politics of Neo-Nationalism
The Christian Right and Secular Nationalism in America
Jeffrey Haynes

Russian Public Diplomacy
From USSR to the Russian Federation
Marina M. Lebedeva

International Perspectives on Public Administration
Henry T. Sardaryan

Value Chains Transformation and Transport Reconnection in Eurasia
Geo-economic and Geopolitical Implications
Jacopo Maria Pepe

For more information about this series, please visit: www.routledge.com/Innovations-in-International-Affairs/book-series/IIA

Russian Public Diplomacy
From USSR to the Russian Federation

Marina M. Lebedeva

LONDON AND NEW YORK

First published 2021
by Routledge
2 Park Square, Milton Park, Abingdon, Oxon OX14 4RN

and by Routledge
605 Third Avenue, New York, NY 10158

Routledge is an imprint of the Taylor & Francis Group, an informa business

© 2021 Marina M. Lebedeva

The right of Marina M. Lebedeva to be identified as author of this work has been asserted by her in accordance with sections 77 and 78 of the Copyright, Designs and Patents Act 1988.

All rights reserved. No part of this book may be reprinted or reproduced or utilised in any form or by any electronic, mechanical, or other means, now known or hereafter invented, including photocopying and recording, or in any information storage or retrieval system, without permission in writing from the publishers.

Trademark notice: Product or corporate names may be trademarks or registered trademarks, and are used only for identification and explanation without intent to infringe.

British Library Cataloguing-in-Publication Data
A catalogue record for this book is available from the British Library

Library of Congress Cataloging-in-Publication Data
Names: Lebedeva, Marina Mikhaĭlovna, author.
Title: Russian public diplomacy : from USSR to the Russian Federation / Marina M. Lebedeva.
Description: Abingdon, Oxon ; New York, NY : Routledge, 2021. | Series: Innovations in international affairs | Includes bibliographical references and index.
Identifiers: LCCN 2020053810 (print) | LCCN 2020053811 (ebook) | ISBN 9780367708740 (hardback) | ISBN 9781003148319 (ebook)
Subjects: LCSH: Russia (Federation)—Relations. | Russia (Federation)—Foreign public opinion.
Classification: LCC DK510.764 .L433 2021 (print) | LCC DK510.764 (ebook) | DDC 327.47—dc23
LC record available at https://lccn.loc.gov/2020053810
LC ebook record available at https://lccn.loc.gov/2020053811

ISBN: 978-0-367-70874-0 (hbk)
ISBN: 978-0-367-70876-4 (pbk)
ISBN: 978-1-003-14831-9 (ebk)

Typeset in Times New Roman
by Apex CoVantage, LLC

Contents

1 Introduction: the transforming modern world and public diplomacy — 1

2 Public diplomacy and the reasons for its development in the world in the 21st century — 3

3 Formation and development of Russian public diplomacy — 14

4 Russian studies of public diplomacy in the 2000s — 27

5 Conclusion — 49

References — 52
Index — 68

1 Introduction
The transforming modern world and public diplomacy

The modern world is undergoing drastic changes. This fact is reflected both in the speeches of political leaders from various countries of the world and in the academic literature. However, the question of what exactly is being transformed remains debatable. Most researchers proceed from the assumption that the transformation of the modern world is due to changes in interstate relations after the end of the Cold War [see, e.g., Kissinger, 2014]. Indeed, interstate relations are changing, being an important structural element of the political organization of the world. But this is not the only element that is changing. Political transformation in the modern world covers at least three levels of the political organization of the world: (1) the Westphalian system [see Keohane & Nye, 1971]; (2) the system of interstate relations; and (3) the political systems of various countries, many of which have undergone changes at the turn of the 20th and 21st centuries. The transformation of each level intensifies the changes taking place in the other two. As a result, the phenomenon of the "perfect storm" is formed [Lebedeva, 2016]. Changes in the political organization of the world mean that an increasing number of actors are involved in public diplomacy, and the tool of public diplomacy is becoming more important for states.

Simultaneously with changes in the political organization of the world, the role of social and humanitarian resources and, consequently, their means of influence, increases [Lebedeva, 2018]. This is due to the importance of the human factor and human capital in the modern world. It is the human being who is now at the center of economic, social, and political development. Many researchers, including Russian ones, pay attention to this aspect [see, e.g., Gromoglasova, 2018; Zonova, 2004].

In addition, the strengthening of the role of social and humanitarian resources is associated with the development of communication and information technologies, which make it possible for billions of people to search for and obtain information, as well as communicate. As a result, in the practical sphere, much attention has been paid to the problems of health, tourism, the fight against poverty, etc. Accordingly, in the scientific field, the number of studies in the humanitarian and social fields is increasing, and concepts that are directly related to the social and humanitarian spheres are appearing (in particular, the concept of "soft power" by Nye [2002]). Of course, military-political and political-economic resources do not reduce their "weight" in world politics. In this case, we are talking about the fact that social and humanitarian means of influence become no less effective than other means. Moreover, social and humanitarian means "connect" to other means of influence, including military ones, often reinforcing them. An example of this is hybrid wars, when various means of influencing the enemy are used, as well as propaganda, fake news, etc.

Public diplomacy develops in the context of changes in world politics and under the influence of these changes. Because public diplomacy is a part of a social and humanitarian resource, its role in the modern world as a means of influence increases dramatically. At the same time, along with public diplomacy, other tools related to social and humanitarian impact are widely used throughout the world, including propaganda, strategic communication, and the formation of national branding. All states use the entire arsenal of tools for influence. In this case, the focus of analysis is precisely public diplomacy. At the same time, it is essential to highlight the characteristic features of public diplomacy that distinguish it from other tools.

Russia is currently active on the world stage. The analysis of Russian public diplomacy will allow us to better understand how various state and non-state structures are involved in shaping the world's perceptions by Russian public diplomacy and its implementation.

Finally, there is another reason for the interest in Russia and, in particular, Russian public diplomacy. The world is becoming more and more complex, and non-Western states and citizens of the non-Western world are actively involved in it. This explains the increased interest that is now shown in non-Western approaches, concepts, and theories [see, e.g., Acharya, 2016].

In recent years, articles on Russian public diplomacy have appeared, written mainly by foreign scholars. In this case, the focus of attention is on Russian public diplomacy – how it is built and studied within Russia. The book emphasizes public diplomacy in general and particularly in Russia. The public diplomacy toolkit is largely universal. However, how it is applied, which technologies are primarily used, and how public diplomacy is combined with other means of influence are specific to each state.

The concept of "public diplomacy" came to Russia, as well as to many other countries, from the English-language literature. Therefore, before considering Russian public diplomacy, it is important to analyze what is generally understood by public diplomacy.

2 Public diplomacy and the reasons for its development in the world in the 21st century

Public diplomacy: definition and understanding

Public diplomacy, along with soft power issues, has become one of the most discussed topics in world politics and, in particular, in the theory of diplomacy. Both theoretical issues and the practice of using public diplomacy in various countries [see, e.g., *The New Public Diplomacy*..., 2005], including Russia [see, e.g., Simons, 2014], are studied. Public diplomacy is becoming an integral part of world politics, and its analysis makes it possible to better understand both world politics itself and the foreign policy of various countries. However, public diplomacy is understood in different ways. Russia is no exception in this regard.

The concept of public diplomacy,[1] which appeared in the United States in the middle of the 20th century at the Fletcher School of Law and Diplomacy at Tufts University thanks to E. Gullion, is defined as follows:

> Public diplomacy deals with the influence of public attitudes on the formation and execution of foreign policies . . . encompasses dimensions of foreign relations beyond traditional diplomacy, the cultivation by governments of public opinion in other countries; the interaction of private groups and interests in one country with those of another.[2]

A similar definition is given by the US Department of State: "Public diplomacy refers to government-sponsored programs intended to inform or influence public opinion in other countries; its chief instruments are publications, motion pictures, cultural exchanges, radio and television" [*Dictionary*..., 1987].

In turn, the book edited by Snow and Taylor describes public diplomacy as the impact of one state on the society of another (other) state [*Routledge Handbook of Public Diplomacy*, 2008]. A close definition is given by the Russian researcher A. V. Dolinskiy. He proposes to understand public diplomacy as a means by which the government of one country tries to influence the society of another so that it, in turn, affects its government [Dolinskiy, 2013a]. Thus, in fact, the definition of public diplomacy as the impact of the state on the societies of foreign countries has become widespread.

From the previous definitions it follows that, first, public diplomacy is an activity carried out or directed by the state, and second, the channels for implementing public diplomacy can be twofold: through officials (e.g., a representative of a state department to hold a press conference for foreign journalists) and through non-state actors (nongovernmental organizations [NGOs], universities, theaters, etc.) [Lebedeva, 2017b]. The main emphasis, however, is often placed on non-state actors.

Initially, US public diplomacy was focused on countering communist propaganda. In this regard, American scholars usually contrasted public diplomacy with the activities of the USSR in the international arena. In the 1990s, interest in public diplomacy declined significantly, since the end of the collapse of the USSR gave rise to the illusion of the end of any significant value contradictions in the world, which was most clearly reflected in Fukuyama's article on the end of history [1989]. The beginning of the 21st century was marked by the revival of public diplomacy in the world. In many ways, the United States initiated this revival. There are several reasons for the new stage in the development of public diplomacy. First of all, the terrorist attacks of 9/11 showed that the value contradictions in the world have not disappeared. The reaction of many people in the Middle East to the attacks on 9/11 made clear that millions of people had a negative perception of US policy. Obviously, it was impossible to correct the negative image of the United States only by means of traditional diplomacy. To solve this problem, representatives of the American elite again turned to the means of public diplomacy. Therefore, having experienced a decline in the 1990s under the influence of the illusion of "the end of history", public diplomacy was revived with renewed vigor after the tragedy of 9/11 [Melissen, 2005; Dolinskiy, 2011a].

At the same time, at the beginning of the 21st century, other reasons for turning to the tools of public diplomacy are directly due to the processes of transformation of the political organization of the world, especially the Westphalian system. Thus, the development of communication and information technologies has led to a sharp intensification of interaction between people in the world beyond their national borders. As a result, non-state actors entered the world arena en masse and joined public diplomacy as its subjects and objects.

In the 21st century, not only has the number of non-state actors in the world increased significantly [Gotz, 2011], but their interaction with states also increased. Social and humanitarian resources are increasingly being used by states to influence foreign audiences. Finally, Nye's concept of soft power, centered on the idea of attractiveness [1990], played its role in the revival of public diplomacy.

New public diplomacy and propaganda

New realities of the 21st century – the development of communication and information technologies; a sharp surge in the activity of non-state actors due to the opportunities that these technologies have opened up; blurred boundaries between internal and external information spaces, etc. – all led to the creation of a new public diplomacy, the name of which has been fixed in scientific research [see, e.g., *The New Public Diplomacy* . . . , 2005; Cull, 2009]. In addition, public diplomacy has become widespread outside the United States: it covers almost all countries of the world, including Russia.

New phenomena have also appeared in public diplomacy. If earlier public diplomacy was considered as a means of only the state, nowadays public diplomacy is becoming a means of influence of international organizations and unions. Melissen wrote in 2005 that public diplomacy is developing. And in the modern world, the European Union and the UN are successfully demonstrating the capabilities of supranational public diplomacy in action [Melissen, 2005].

One more important point characterizes the modern new public diplomacy: it involves not just influencing the society of another state, but also interacting with it, that is, through dialogue [Melissen, 2005]. An indication of dialogue as a distinctive feature of public diplomacy is also contained in the study by Russian authors Kornilov and Makarychev, who write, "soft power is not a unilateral tool to coerce others and in this respect it differs from hard power or propaganda" [2015, p. 239].

The manifestation of this dialogue is observed through the official and unofficial channels of the implementation of public diplomacy. It is no accident that social networks have developed rapidly in the framework of public diplomacy. Of course, there are many examples of public diplomacy where such a dialogue is absent. But then the question arises about its effectiveness in modern conditions.

As an attribute of public diplomacy, it is also indicated that traditional diplomacy was characterized by the interaction between the state and society (government to people, or G2P), while the new diplomacy was the interaction between people from different countries (people to people, or P2P) [Snow, 2010]. In addition, such a characteristic of new public diplomacy as the use of network interaction openness is noted [Zaharna, 2007].

Due to the emergence of the concept of soft power, public diplomacy has become seen as a tool of soft power and in this sense has become a counter to propaganda [see, e.g., *The New Public Diplomacy* . . . , 2005]. However, propaganda, as well as public diplomacy, involves influencing the audience. Thus, Jowett and O'Donnel emphasize that propaganda and beliefs are used interchangeably. Propaganda, in the most neutral sense, means to disseminate or promote particular ideas. In Latin, it means "to propagate" or "to sow" [Jowett & O'Donnel, 2012, p. 2].

As a result, it turns out that the definition of public diplomacy as given earlier does not contradict this definition of propaganda. From this, one can conclude that the emergence of the concept of public diplomacy, in fact, did not bring anything new. However, it did. As Melissen notes, diplomacy has nothing to do with propaganda [2005]. Indeed, in studies of diplomacy, it is rare to find references to propaganda, in contrast to journalistic articles on diplomacy. In the same study, Melissen writes, "public diplomacy is similar to propaganda in that it tries to persuade people what to think, but it is fundamentally different from it in the sense that public diplomacy also listens to what people have to say" [2005, p. 18]. These are important differences between propaganda and public diplomacy. At the same time, it seems that these are not the main differences. The key question is how to implement such an impact on the external auditors. And here another concept comes to aid – the concept of soft power by Nye [1990], which appeared much later than the concept of public diplomacy expressed by Gullion at the Fletcher School of Law and Diplomacy in the 1960s. It is no coincidence that the term "propaganda" is often used with negative connotations, and recently it has often been used in conjunction with the concept of "fake news" [see, e.g., Tandoc, Zheng, & Ling, 2017].

Thus, public diplomacy is an instrument of soft power, as described by Nye [2008]. However, first, the fact that Nye's concept appears much later than the concept and definition of Gullion misleads many scholars, which sometimes gives rise to the identification of public diplomacy with propaganda. Second, in practical terms, states always use propaganda focused on hard power, as well as public diplomacy, which is based on soft power. That is why Nye introduced the concept of "smart power".

As a result, many authors now assume that public diplomacy is not the same as propaganda, since it means greater openness [Zaharna, 2004] and does not involve disinformation. The technologies of public diplomacy primarily presuppose openness, dialogue with foreign audiences, and the formation of attractiveness.

Propaganda does not mean focusing on attractiveness. Moreover, propaganda does not exclude the use of various options for manipulating people's minds, which, in essence, is not allowed by soft power. This clearly shows the difference between the neoliberal approach to international relations, in the framework of which Nye mainly works, and the realist approach, which implies fierce rivalry between states in the international arena on which propaganda is based.

There is no difference between propaganda and soft power in the realist approach. Perhaps the most striking difference between realism and neoliberalism in relation to soft power and propaganda approaches is demonstrated by Knight. She writes that Nye's concept became very popular: both political leaders and representatives of academia pounced on her "like bees on honey".[3] However, she further erroneously ascribes to Nye a realistic position. Knight argues that the basis of any force, whether it is "soft" or "hard", are countries' own interests, and this manifests itself, in her view, as a focus on realism. For this reason, the Knight asks the question, is not Nye's soft power a form of manifestation of domination and realization of the state's own interests? Knight describes two situations, assuming that both belong to the realist approach. The first situation presupposes a desire to realize only one's own interests. The second situation involves taking into account the partner's interests. In principle, the second situation is incorporated in Nye's concept, although it is not clearly defined by him. Hence, the concept of "soft power" introduced by Nye is interpreted by various researchers and politicians very broadly, often in a way that contradicts what Nye meant.

At the same time, it cannot be said that propaganda is an ineffective means of influencing the public opinion of foreign countries, as well as realistically oriented behavior in general. In some situations, especially when it is necessary to quickly achieve the desired result from the opposite side, propaganda and even methods such as pressure and blackmail can be effective means. Otherwise, propaganda would not be applied at all. Another thing is that it is unlikely that propaganda influence can last long. There is a principle that is formulated in a well-known expression regarding the fact that one can come to power on bayonets, but it is difficult to hold onto it. The correlation of the characteristics of soft power and propaganda can be schematically represented as in Table 2.1 [Lebedeva, 2017a] (more parameters, of course, can be added).

It should be emphasized that the proposed dichotomy of public diplomacy as a tool of soft power, on the one hand, and propaganda, on the other, is not absolute. Moreover, Nye, contrasting soft power with hard power, nevertheless speaks of a continuum of means of influence. He illustrates his point graphically, where hard power is on the left and soft power is on the right. Both types of power connect a single line [Nye, 2004a]. Obviously, the boundaries of the two types of "power" are "blurred". In practice, soft power in the form of public diplomacy and hard power in the form

Table 2.1 Correlations between characteristics of propaganda and public diplomacy

Propaganda	Public diplomacy, understood as an instrument of soft power
1 Allows imposition (coercion), as well as various types of incentives (rewards)	1 Does not permit imposition or stimulation (the opposite side has to make its choice)
2 Used in the framework of realism (attention only to one's own interests)	2 Used in the framework of neoliberalism (including attention to the interests of another)
3 Most likely will not work in the long run	3 Focuses on long-term interaction with a partner
4 Uses manipulative strategies	4 Avoids using manipulative strategies
5 Focused on the monologue; perceives the opposite side as an object	5 Focused on the dialogue; perceives the opposite side as a subject
6 Building trust is not a focus of attention	6 Involves the creation of a trusting relationship

of propaganda are often used simultaneously in relation to the same subject. However, the question arises as to the advantages and limitations of such simultaneous use of soft power in the form of public diplomacy and propaganda.

Public diplomacy, sharp power, and strategic communication

Blurring the boundaries between soft power and hard power gives rise to attempts to create new terms such as, in particular, sharp power [Walker & Ludwig, 2017]. According to Walker and Ludwig, for example, the use of cultural and educational programs by authoritarian regimes cannot be considered either soft power or hard power, since these actions are not aimed at creating attractiveness but at undermining the foundations of democratic countries. A similar rebuke aimed at changing the political regime is essentially put forward by the opposite side, which accuses Western countries of color revolutions. It is noteworthy that Nye, who entered into the discussion regarding sharp power, also noted that, in principle, it is rather difficult to determine the boundaries between soft power and sharp power. However, "if we use the term 'sharp power' as a shorthand for information warfare, the contrast with soft power becomes obvious. Sharp power is a type of hard power" [Nye, 2018].

In recent years, the concept of "strategic communication" has gained popularity in the academic literature. Public diplomacy has often become synonymous with strategic communication. Nye, considering the connection between soft power and public diplomacy, writes about the importance of strategic communication [2008]. At the same time, he agrees with the understanding of strategic communication proposed by Leonard. Leonard drew attention to the fact that many organizations and agencies dealing with politics, trade, culture, and so on interact with the external auditor based on their institutional and corporate interests. However, the external audience must have a holistic image about the other country; therefore, strategic communication is a set of activities [Leonard, 2002]. Indeed, the idea of a holistic image is important in terms of influencing the audience. However, this is possible only if a significant degree of hierarchical relations exist in the state, which was, for example, the case in the Soviet Union. Therefore, non-state or semi-state "structures-conductors" could create a holistic image, and they often acted very successfully. The modern world is increasingly built according to the network principle. Influence of the state on foreign societies takes place not only through non-state actors that are "conductors", but also through more independent structures that are actors of world politics. To a large extent, they independently implement ideas that are in line with state policy. Another thing is that complex questions arise about the actor nature of non-state structures in the framework of public diplomacy: to what extent do they consciously form the image of the state abroad, or is this a by-product of their activities? In the face of a huge number of non-state actors, how can it be possible and is it possible to regulate their activities? And if during the Cold War, when public diplomacy was highly state supervised [Dolinskiy, 2011b], the question of the independence of the behavior of non-state actors of public diplomacy was not actually raised, today it is not so.

At the same time, the hierarchy of relations remains in the military sphere. The army of any state is built according to the type of hierarchy. It is no coincidence that the problem of strategic communication began to be developed in the North Atlantic Treaty Organization (NATO). For example, the NATO Strategic Communications Centre of Excellence, a NATO-accredited international military organization, quite broadly defines strategic communications, which includes public diplomacy, public affairs, military public affairs, information operations, and psychological operations.[4]

Formally, this understanding of public diplomacy, as well as the concept of propaganda, fits the definitions of public diplomacy given earlier. However, it seems that the concepts of public diplomacy and strategic communication are not identical. Strategic communication includes not only public diplomacy, but also other types of influence. These types of influence can be quite severe and fall under the definition of propaganda or information wars.

An important factor that influenced the popularity of strategic communication among the military was not only the hierarchical organization of military structures, but also the fact that another level of the political organization of the world [Lebedeva, 2016] – the system of international (interstate) relations – after 30 years has not taken shape (another question was, how possible was its design?). The result was an intensified confrontation between states in the international arena. And this, in turn, led to the active inclusion of the information component in this confrontation. As a result, we are seeing a large number of information wars in the modern world. Thus, despite the fact that public diplomacy is defined in different ways and, according to the widespread definition of it, does not exclude propaganda at all, the fundamental difference between strategic communication and public diplomacy is in the latter's orientation towards soft power, the key point of which is attractiveness. At the same time, in a number of Russian studies, public diplomacy is associated with strategic communication.

It should be noted that the mere presence of attractiveness does not mean that this attractiveness is perceived by others. Soft power is only a potential that can be used, and it can only remain as a potential. The presence of attractiveness must still be disclosed, and must be shown to the other side. For this reason, Panova, following constructivist ideas, argues that creating attractiveness as a necessary condition for exercising soft power is nothing more than a linguistic construction of an interpretation of reality" [Panova, 2012: 15]. Another thing is that the special task is how to create this attraction. One of the important elements for creating attractiveness is the presence of a trusting relationship [Kononenko, 2006]. Its absence initially leads to suspicion and, eventually, a neutral or even negative perception. However, another situation is not excluded when the objective presence of attractiveness is not emphasized. In this case, the potential can become attractive on its own without any effort or action.

Another important point is that attractiveness is not a universal characteristic. It is obvious that any society is heterogeneous. One social group is attracted to one thing, while another is attracted to another one. Therefore, there can be no universal attractiveness, or in other words, universal soft power, and, therefore, universal public diplomacy. Public diplomacy aimed at one social group may be perceived by another social group with a different value system as propaganda.

Public diplomacy and national branding

If the ideas of strategic communication are largely associated with research in the military sphere, then from the field of marketing came the idea of public diplomacy as an activity that creates the brand of the state. One of the main roles here was played by Anholt, who introduced the term "national branding" and then came to the conclusion that public diplomacy is only a part of national branding. He wrote, "I have always intended Nation Branding to consider how the nation as a whole presents and represents itself to other nations, whereas PD appears to concentrate exclusively on the presentation and representation of government policy to other publics" [2006, p. 271]. This understanding of public diplomacy also raises a number of questions. First, Anholt sees the activities of non-state actors only as "conductors" of state policy, depriving them of their independence. Unfortunately, the questions about the actor nature of non-state structures and their independence and interaction (or lack of interaction) with the state in the framework of public diplomacy have not yet received due theoretical understanding.

Second, the brand aims not only to make a product attractive, but also to sell it. Public diplomacy does not always involve the latter, although there are some areas that involve selling, such as tourism. However, in this case, the commercial side appears. In addition, it is relatively easy to abandon a product brand for one reason or another. It can be changed. The national image is focused on the long term and its replacement is difficult.

Third, creating a brand does not involve a dialogue. The brand is offered to the buyer, but the seller does not enter into discussions with the buyer regarding the brand. At best, the seller collects the buyer's opinions in order to further develop the brand. It is a different matter in the case of public diplomacy, when representatives of official structures and non-state "conductors" and actors in most cases directly (or indirectly through social networks, chat rooms, etc.) interact with representatives of foreign society.

The main characteristics of public diplomacy

Thus, due to the cardinal changes that have taken place in the world since the middle of the last century, the definition of public diplomacy as the influence of the state directly or indirectly through non-state actors on the foreign audience began to include many different instruments of influence. In practice, all states use this toolkit in various combinations, paying little attention to the accuracy of the name of one or another instrument of influence. The same thing is happening in the scientific sphere. At present, as a result of the restructuring of interstate relations, which did not take shape after the end of the Cold War, international relations and international studies are becoming extremely ideologized and politicized. As a result, fake news is widely used in the practice of interaction, and public diplomacy is identified with propaganda. Therefore, it seems to be extremely important to distinguish between different instruments of influence on foreign audiences.

Thus, the distinguishing features of public diplomacy from other instruments of influence are:

1 In practical terms,

- Creation of attractiveness and taking into account the interests of a foreign audience
- Focus on cooperation and dialogue with foreign audiences
- Openness in relationships
- Orientation to the foreign policy of the state implementing public diplomacy

2 In theoretical terms,

- Focus on the concept of soft power
- Using a neoliberal or constructivist theory

Any actions related to influencing an external audience and not meeting these criteria cannot be considered public diplomacy. Of course, there are a number of characteristics that define the new public diplomacy, including networking, P2P communication, and others. These are important characteristics of modern public diplomacy, but they are not criteria that distinguish public diplomacy from other instruments of state influence on foreign societies and, rather, characterize its current state, as well as the effectiveness of influence.

In Russia, as in other countries, sometimes no distinction is made between the various instruments of influencing the external audience. This causes many problems. Thus, public diplomacy, when evaluated by various Russian and foreign authors, is often identified with other instruments of influencing an external audience through propaganda and strategic communication. However, these are different means of influence and require separate consideration. Thus, according to the selected criteria, neither propaganda nor strategic communication is public diplomacy. The situation is more complicated when public diplomacy is used, but due to the strong ideologization and politicization of modern international relations, it is interpreted as propaganda. The problem of possible variants of impact interpretation requires a separate theoretical development. In this case, when considering public diplomacy in Russia, I will proceed, first, from the specified criteria of public diplomacy, and second, from how public diplomacy is understood and studied in Russia, but not how these actions are interpreted and can be perceived outside of Russia by various groups of the population, as well as by the governments of different countries or by various researchers, both within Russia and abroad. The interpretation of actions in public diplomacy depends on many political and ideological reasons, as well as social factors. This is a different problem.

Notes

1 The term "public diplomacy" was used earlier. See Cull, N. (2006, April 18). "Public diplomacy" before Gullion: The evolution of a phrase. *USC Center on Public Diplomacy*. Retrieved from www.uscpublicdiplomacy.org/blog/public-diplomacy-gullion-evolution-phrase
2 Edward R. Murrow Center of Public Diplomacy. Retrieved from https://publicdiplomacy.wikia.org/wiki/The_Edward_R._Murrow_Center_of_Public_Diplomacy
3 Knight, J. (2014, January 31). The limits of soft power in higher education. *University World News*. Issue 305. Retrieved from www.universityworldnews.com/article.php?story=20140129134636725
4 NATO Strategic Communications Centre of Excellence. *About Strategic Communications*. Retrieved from https://stratcomcoe.org/about-strategic-communications

3 Formation and development of Russian public diplomacy

Origins of Russian public diplomacy: Soviet period

Russia has not stayed away from the revival of public diplomacy in the 21st century. At the same time, Russian public diplomacy (at the time defined as people's diplomacy) and experience in public diplomacy have their roots in the Soviet period. Public diplomacy of the Soviet time was significantly ideologically oriented. Soviet practice and experience are reflected in the formation and development of Russian public diplomacy, as well as in its current state.

The term "public diplomacy" was not used in the USSR. Instead, another notion was used – "people's diplomacy", which was understood as the activity of scientists, artists, astronauts, and so on that was aimed at creating a positive image of the Soviet Union abroad. Accordingly, public diplomacy was actually limited to the sphere of activities of non-state or formal non-state actors. The activities of official structures in the international arena were not included in the concept of people's diplomacy. However, the ideological basis has disappeared although, of course, public speeches delivered by Soviet officials were often aimed at an external audience.

The question of the attractiveness of a socialist state actually arose from the first days of its existence. After the revolution of 1917, Russia found itself in international isolation. In 1920, international recognition of Russia began. Estonia and the Republic of Latvia were among the first to recognize it. Of particular importance for the international recognition of the USSR was the Genoese Conference in 1922, which was held with the participation of representatives of 29 states and five British dominions. All of this prompted the USSR to establish and develop both diplomacy and public (people's) diplomacy in the country.

As for public diplomacy, in the mid-1920s, the USSR created the All-Union Society for Cultural Relations with Foreign Countries (VOKS), the aim of which was, on the one hand, to popularize the culture of the peoples of the Soviet Union abroad and, on the other hand, to introduce the culture of foreign states to the people of the USSR. Its activities were influenced by similar organizations that were created earlier in the world, such as Alliance Française and others. A certain role in the establishment of VOKS was played by the fact that foreign NGOs for the fight against hunger worked in Russia during this time [Gridnev, 2000]. Such cultural figures as Mayakovsky, Prokofiev, Rolan, Shostakovich, Dreiser, and others took an active part in the work of VOKS.[1]

In 1958, the Union of Soviet Societies for Friendship and Cultural Relations with Foreign Countries (SSOD) was created based on VOKS, and the task was the development of cultural and scientific ties between public organizations, institutions, and individual representatives of science and culture of the USSR and foreign countries.

Scientific ties developed during the Soviet period, primarily within the USSR Academy of Sciences. Soviet scientists were active participants in the Pugwash movement of scientists for peace, disarmament, international security, and the prevention of nuclear war, which began to operate in the 1950s and played a significant role in the prevention of nuclear war. Participants in the Pugwash movement have put forward initiatives to ban nuclear testing, as well to prevent the proliferation of nuclear weapons. Russian scholars were well acquainted with their foreign colleagues in scientific activity, which formed a high level of trust [Ryzhov & Lebedev, 2007]. During the Cold War, there were other formats of interaction between Soviet scientists and their foreign colleagues. For example, the Dartmouth Conferences, which began in 1960 as an informal periodic meeting of Soviet and American scientists, became a de facto channel for information and exchange of views between the USSR and the United States on international security issues. They discussed issues of arms control and disarmament and engaged in cultural and scientific exchanges [Moskovskiy, 2013].

The media became an important tool of public diplomacy during the Soviet time. In 1929, Moscow Radio began to broadcast regularly to foreign countries. The purpose of this radio station was to acquaint foreign audiences with life in Russia and the Russian point of view on various events in the world. Initially, the broadcast language was German, but soon the radio station began to work in French and English, and broadcasting in Chinese began in the 1940s. It is noteworthy that the broadcasting to the Soviet Union of such radio stations as the BBC and the Voice of America was carried out later. Since the late 1970s, the English-language service has been known as Radio Moscow World Service.

Great importance was attached to sports diplomacy in the USSR. In 1980, Moscow hosted the Olympic Games, which were held for the first time in

Eastern Europe. However, these Games were boycotted by more than 60 countries due to the entry of Russian troops into Afghanistan in 1979.

Cultural diplomacy (tours of theaters, exhibitions, etc.) was also used in the Soviet Union. A detailed overview of cultural diplomacy in the USSR, its mechanisms, structures, and activities in the international arena is given in the book edited by Nagornaya titled *Soviet Cultural Diplomacy in the Cold War (1945–1989)* [Soviet Cultural Diplomacy..., 2018]. At the same time, cultural diplomacy is widely understood in this book. It includes sports diplomacy, scientific diplomacy, peacemaking, and so on.

In the later Soviet period, children's people's diplomacy began to develop, representing contacts between children from the USSR and the United States [see, e.g., Mizherikov, 2015], as well as the organization of teleconferences between the USSR and the United States.

Thus, after the collapse of the USSR, Russia had some experience in public diplomacy (people's diplomacy). However, this experience, first, related to the Cold War period – a period of confrontation with the West. Second, public diplomacy in the USSR was highly centralized. It was largely coordinated by the state. Third, despite the fact that certain public diplomacy events could be widely covered by the media, the number of participants in public diplomacy was very limited. For example, young scholars usually remained aloof from activities in the framework of public diplomacy.

Thus, despite the fact that Soviet soft power and public diplomacy differ from modern means of influence, which Tsygankov, in particular, wrote about [2006], in the Soviet time, institutions designed to carry out public diplomacy were formed, and structures and channels of interaction were built with a foreign audience. These institutions were of a state or semi-state nature and involved relatively few Soviet people in their work, since communication between countries during the Cold War was limited not only by ideology, but also by technical possibilities of interaction that are not comparable to modern means of communication. Therefore, the G2P interaction formula was valid for all states at that time, including the USSR.

Russian public diplomacy in the 1990s and early 2000s

The general decline in interest in the instrument of public diplomacy in the 1990s also affected Russia. Nevertheless, some steps were taken to maintain public diplomacy in new Russia during this period. Established in 1992, the Russian Association for International Cooperation (RAMS) became the legal successor of the SSOD.[2] In 1994, the Russian Center for International Scientific and Cultural Cooperation (Roszarubezhtsentr)[3] was created under the Government of the Russian Federation.[4] In 1993, the Decree of President Boris Yeltsin created the broadcasting company Voice of Russia based on Radio Moscow World Service.[5] However, changes in the practice of public diplomacy in Russia in the 1990s did not affect its essential characteristics, which were developed in the Soviet time. Most of the Voice of Russia employees continued to work, but changes were made to the broadcasting. For example, the Chinese editorial office launched a weekly program for businesspeople from the PRC with advice on how to do business in Russia and what legislation was in force in Russia in this area.[6]

In general, the changes in the practice of public diplomacy in Russia in the 1990s did not affect the essential characteristics of public diplomacy that developed during the Soviet period.

Russia returned to the practice of public diplomacy actively in the 2000s. An important factor was the revival of public diplomacy in the world. However, along with this, the reason for Russia's appeal to public diplomacy in the 21st century was its focus on regaining its influence on world politics. This orientation in foreign policy was a kind of reaction to the significant loss of Russia's position on the world stage in the 1990s.

At the same time, the concept of soft power and its applicability to public diplomacy was not immediately accepted by the academic community or by politicians in Russia. The idea of Nye, which he put forward in the early 1990s, was first met with a great deal of skepticism. The most common objection was that Nye's concept did not contain anything new. The reasoning was based on the fact that since the advent of humanity, some groups have somehow "softly" influenced others. In the academic environment, realism was dominant, so it was difficult to distinguish between soft power and propaganda. At the same time, the general background for criticism of Nye's concept was euphoria in relation to the "end of history" and, as a consequence, the absence of any special need to influence public opinion in other countries.

Since the beginning of the 2000s, Russia has taken actions in two directions in order to activate its foreign policy and to strengthen its position on the world stage:

1. The adoption of official strategic documents that fixed the importance of using soft power and public diplomacy in Russia's foreign policy.
2. The formation of a number of structures for the implementation of public diplomacy and the revitalization of their activities. The greatest activity occurred during the second half of the noughties, when the practice of public diplomacy began to develop through two channels: official (e.g., briefings at the Russian Foreign Ministry, websites of the Russian Foreign Ministry and Russian embassies) and unofficial (activity of non-state actors and/or actors associated with the state).

The development of the practice of public diplomacy in the 1990s–early 2000s gave the first impetus to research soft power and public diplomacy in Russia. Discussion of Nye's concept in Russian academic circles was also important in this regard.

Issues of soft power and public diplomacy in the foreign policy concepts of the Russian Federation

Since the 2000s, the issue of public diplomacy and soft power has been reflected in official Russian documents, primarily in such a strategic document as the Russian Foreign Policy Concept, which sets the main directions of Russian foreign policy. Therefore, it is important how they define the place and role of public diplomacy and soft power.

From 2000 to the present, four Russian Foreign Policy Concepts have been adopted. At the same time, the approach to influencing the foreign audience was somewhat specified.

A section on "information support of foreign policy activity" appeared in the Russian Foreign Policy Concept in 2000. This section sets out the task of influencing the societies of foreign countries by bringing objective and accurate information about their positions on major international issues, foreign policy initiatives, and actions of the Russian Federation, as well as the achievements of Russian culture, science, and intellectual creativity to the broad circles of the world community.[7]

The term "public diplomacy" appeared for the first time in the Russian Foreign Policy Concept in 2008. Public diplomacy is understood as an instrument of information support for foreign policy. The Concept emphasizes that Russia will seek its objective perception in the world and develop its own effective means of informational influence on public opinion abroad. At the same time, along with public diplomacy, the Concept used the term "people's diplomacy" as the potential of civil society institutions.[8] Thus, the role of non-state actors was highlighted.

In 2010, the ideas of public diplomacy were developed in a document approved by the president of the Russian Federation: "The Main Directions of Russian Policy in the Field of International Cultural and Humanitarian Cooperation".[9] The document notes that competition in the cultural and civilizational dimension is currently increasing, so there is a need for cultural diplomacy. It is noteworthy that the term "public diplomacy" was not used in it. Instead, this document talked about cultural diplomacy and people's diplomacy, which were understood quite widely, including smoothing international contradictions, promoting modernization, and promoting Russian culture as a product on the world market.

The Foreign Policy Concepts of 2013[10] and of 2016 confirmed the importance of Russian informational influence in the world. Russian Foreign Policy Concept 2016 said,

> Russia seeks to ensure that the world has an objective image of the country, develops its own effective ways to influence foreign audiences, promotes Russian and Russian-language media in the global information space, providing them with necessary government support, is proactive in international information cooperation, and takes necessary steps to counter threats to its information security.[11]

In addition, the 2016 Concept puts a special emphasis on cultural identity of the peoples of Russia and Russian education and research as well as consolidation of the Russian-speaking diaspora.[12]

The term "soft power" appears in the 2013 Foreign Policy Concept. It says,

> "Soft power", a comprehensive toolkit for achieving foreign policy objectives building on civil society potential, information, cultural and other methods and technologies alternative to traditional diplomacy, is becoming an indispensable component of modern international relations. At the same time, increasing global competition and the growing crisis potential sometimes creates a risk of destructive and unlawful use of "soft power" and human rights concepts to exert political pressure on sovereign states, interfere in their internal affairs, destabilize their political situation, manipulate public opinion, including under the pretext of financing cultural and human rights projects abroad.[13]

This understanding of soft power shows a wary perception of this concept. However, in the 2016 Foreign Policy Concept, soft power is already defined the following way:

> "soft power" has become an integral part of efforts to achieve foreign policy objectives. This primarily includes the tools offered by civil society, as well as various methods and technologies – from information and communication, to humanitarian and other types.[14]

In general, in the 21st century, Russian official documents clearly trace Russia's desire to use public diplomacy to build its positive image abroad using soft power, which is understood quite widely as non-force impact. At the same time, soft power is widely understood in documents as a non-forceful influence.

Reforming old structures in the field of public diplomacy, creating new ones, and developing their activity

The course taken in official documents on the use of public diplomacy means was reflected in the development of appropriate structures for its implementation. On the one hand, existing structures were reformed, and on the other, a whole series of new ones were created. Among the structures that have been reformed, and that should be highlighted, include the media, such as Voice of Russia and RIA-Novosti. In addition, according to the Decree of President V. Putin in 2002, Russian foreign centers of cultural and scientific cooperation were transferred from the jurisdiction of the Government of the Russian Federation to the Ministry of Foreign Affairs of Russia in order to improve coordination of work.[15]

In 2008, based on Roszarubezhtsentr, according to the Decree of the President of Russia, the Federal Agency for the Commonwealth of Independent States, was created for compatriots living abroad and for international humanitarian cooperation (Rossotrudnichestvo),focusing on issues of supporting the Russian language and culture and interaction with compatriots.[16] At the beginning of 2020, Rossotrudnichestvo was represented in 80 countries by 97 representative offices: 73 Russian centers of science and culture in 62 countries and 24 representatives of the agency in embassies in 21 countries.[17] The results of activities and coordination work are annually reflected in the reports of Rossotrudnichestvo, which formulate the main emphases of the Russian policy of cultural and humanitarian cooperation with other countries. The last such document was released in 2019 and presented the results of activities for 2018.[18]

In general, the Russian academic literature positively assesses the activities of Rossotrudnichestvo [see, e.g., Morozov & Simons, 2020]. At the same time, criticism of this organization is also given. For example, Achkasova and Kostritskaya note that Rossotrudnichestvo has lost the mechanisms and technologies of interaction that existed for the spread of the Russian language and culture in the Soviet era [Achkasova & Kostritskaya, 2014].

As for the state direction in the field of public diplomacy, government agencies working abroad and with foreign audiences (the Ministry of Foreign Affairs of Russia, embassies, consulates, and others) began to create their own websites. They provide information in social networks also. Official structures, both in Russia and abroad, use social networks and websites to varying degrees and with different effects.

A number of new structures have been formed. In the field of mass media, one of the most striking phenomena was the creation of the foreign broadcasting channel Russia Today (later RT) in 2005. The task of the channel was to provide information about Russia, as well as to give a Russian perspective on world events. In principle, as far as the task is concerned, there was nothing new here in comparison with radio broadcasting. At first, the channel was broadcast in English, and then in Arabic, Spanish, and French. The concept of the channel changed as it developed. As Dolinskiy notes,

> At first, the channel attempted to do BBC-style. . . . Then it switched to a regional focus on the former Soviet Union, following the model of Al Jazeera. . . . Finally, the channel developed a policy of broadcasting "alternative" news that escape major networks and contradict the mainstream.
>
> [2013b]

In addition to creating a television channel, a new format of influencing the societies of foreign countries with the help of newspaper materials has appeared. *Rossiyskaya Gazeta* began to publish monthly tabs to such foreign publications as *The Daily Telegraph, Washington Post*, and *Le Figaro*, as well as to leading publications of Argentina, Brazil, India, Italy, and other countries.

In 2013, based on a Decree of the President of the Russian Federation, the RIA Novosti news agency was liquidated and the international news agency Rossiya Segodnya was created on its basis.[19] In addition, based on the same decree, the Sputnik Agency was created to replace the Voice of Russia radio station. The goals of such changes were described as improving the efficiency of work, including in terms of funding,[20] and strengthening the international component of broadcasting.[21]

In the 2000s, a number of funds were established. The Alexander Gorchakov Public Diplomacy Fund was created based on the decision of the president of Russia.[22] Among the fund's tasks are to promote the formation of a favorable public opinion for Russia abroad; to promote social, cultural, educational, scientific, and management programs in the field of international relations and others; to promote the intellectual, cultural, scientific, and business potential of Russia; and to participate in the educational process and other activities.[23] The fund implements a large number of scientific and educational programs, including the Balkan, Baltic, and Caucasian Dialogues, as well as the Dialogue for the Future. They involve both civil society representatives and retired diplomats.

Another fund created in 2007 based on the Decree of the President of Russia was the Russkiy Mir Foundation.[24] One of the most important goals of the fund was to popularize the Russian language, which is an important element of Russian and world culture, as well as to support programs for studying the Russian language abroad.[25] The fund is financed both from its budget and from private organizations. The year 2007 was declared as the year of the Russian language. The presidential address to the Federal Assembly talked about developing the Russian language in the country, supporting programs of its study in the near and far abroad, and, in general, promoting Russian language and literature throughout the world.[26]

Along with such large funds as the Gorchakov Fund and the Russkiy Mir Foundation in Russia, a number of small organizations can be attributed to NGOs involved in public diplomacy. Among them are organizations that should fall under the term "creative diplomacy", promoted by N. V. Burlinova.

Russia has begun to pay a lot of attention to international sports competitions, seeing in this not only opportunities for public diplomacy but also improving the health of the country's population. Great importance has been attached to the holding of major sporting events in Russia, such as the 2014 Sochi Olympic Games and the 2018 FIFA World Cup. The Universiade in Kazan in 2013 and a number of other events were also significant events in this regard. They are among the means of Russian public diplomacy. In general, sports diplomacy, like cultural diplomacy, has traditions that go back to the Soviet period. Various sports programs are now widely used. Also, master's programs in sports diplomacy began to appear in Russian universities that are focused on training managers in the sports field who are capable of representing the interests of Russian sports in the world sports arena.[27]

Until the beginning of the 21st century, Russia almost did not pay attention to working with compatriots living abroad. After the adoption of the Federal Law on the State Policy of the Russian Federation in relation to compatriots abroad in 1999,[28] the situation has started to change fundamentally. The concept of "compatriot" is widely understood in Russia. It includes not only Russian citizens, but also individuals who share common language, history, cultural heritage, traditions, and customs with Russians, as well as descendants of these individuals. According to 2010 data, over 30 million compatriots lived outside of Russia, most of them in the territory of the states of the former USSR.[29] In May 2011, by Decree of the President of Russia, a Fund for Support and Protection of the Rights of Compatriots Living Abroad was created.[30] The purpose of the fund is to provide Russian compatriots with legal and other necessary support.[31]

In the 2000s, Russia paid close attention to such resources of public diplomacy as higher education and academic exchanges. One of the reasons for this is that during the Soviet period, education and science were the most important areas of foreign relations of the USSR. Students from many developing countries studied in the USSR. In 1960, the Peoples' Friendship University (now the Russian Peoples' Friendship University – RUDN University[32]) was established to train specialists, primarily for countries in

Asia, Africa, and Latin America. In addition, Russian higher education in the world in a number of areas, in particular applied mathematics, physics, and a number of others, is competitive. Also, for example, education in the field of medicine is attractive for students from a number of countries, in particular from India, in terms of price and quality.

In Russia, after the disintegration of the Soviet Union, the number of foreign students dropped sharply as a result of funding problems for higher education, as well as the outflow of university professors and their transition to business. At the same time, in the 21st century, the processes of internationalization of education begin to develop at a rapid pace in the world. As a result, Europe launched the Bologna Process aimed at harmonizing higher education. Russia did not stand aside from the processes of internationalization of higher education. In 2003, Russia joined the Bologna Process. The country switched to a two-stage system of training in higher education – bachelor's and master's degrees. Double diploma master's degrees were created in various areas of training, student exchange programs were increased, and so on. A few years later, Russia adopted the "Concept of Export of Educational Services of the Russian Federation for the Period 2011–2020", which defines the main goals and objectives of the Russian Federation in the field of providing educational services to foreign citizens in Russia and abroad.[33] Russia is also taking a number of measures to develop national education, including adopting the National Education Project, which aims to "ensure the global competitiveness of Russian education and make the Russian Federation one of the top 10 countries in the world for the quality of general education",[34] and increasing funding for education.

Education, along with science and culture, perhaps to the greatest extent presupposes not only impact but interaction and dialogue [Lebedeva & Fort, 2009]. Russia's accession to the Bologna Process in 2003 greatly expanded the possibilities of student exchanges. According to UNESCO, the number of Russian students enrolled in mobility programs in 2017 was more than 250,000.[35] In turn, the number of foreign students in Russia in 2017 was about 278,000 [Ovchinnikova, Zotkina, & Getmanskaya, 2019]. Students from The Commonwealth of Independent States (CIS), Baltic countries, and Georgia in 2018 accounted for approximately 75% of all foreign students studying in Russia.[36] Many students from the CIS speak Russian and therefore do not have a language barrier to study at Russian universities.

To strengthen cooperation with the countries of integration entities that include Russia – the CIS, Brazil, Russia, India, China, and South Africa (BRICS), and The Shanghai Cooperation Organisation (SCO) – network universities have been established. The network university includes several universities that have entered into partnerships and provide students with the opportunity to study at a partner university for a certain period of time.

These universities are the universities of the CIS, SCO, and BRICS, respectively. The issues of organizing network universities are discussed in Russia [see, e.g., Kovalenko & Smolik, 2014].

Interaction between Russian scientists and their foreign colleagues has also increased significantly. If in the Soviet period these were only individual researchers' contacts of those who achieved significant success in science, now international contacts affect almost everyone involved in science. New formats of public diplomacy with the participation of researchers have appeared. This is largely due to the development of modern information and communication technologies. For example, the Trianon Dialogue was created, which was initiated in 2017 by the presidents of Russia and France. The Trianon Dialogue is an interaction between civil societies of the two countries based on a digital platform that combines a portal and a social network. Scientists, including university rectors, participate in this dialogue. Urban and educational issues were the first topics of discussion in the Trianon Dialogue.[37]

In the field of cultural diplomacy, touring and exhibition activities developed. New formats have also appeared. For example, the Children's Musical Theater of the Young Actor (DMTUA), founded in 1988 by the Honored Artist of Russia Alexander Fedorov in 2004, initiated and became one of the founders of the Prologue Children's Theater Festival. Despite the fact that the festival was originally national, it had international resonance.

The Russian Orthodox Church (ROC) has stepped up its international activities. Among the steps taken by the church were the following: a meeting in 1995 with the then UN Secretary General B. Boutros-Ghali and a speech by the patriarch at the European office of the UN, dedicated to the role of the church in overcoming ethnic strife; in 2002, a meeting with the leadership of various structures of the European Union and confirmation of the readiness of the Russian Orthodox Church to participate in a broad ideological dialogue with international structures aimed at creating a multipolar and multi-structured world order; and a number of others.

It should be noted that in order to influence a foreign audience, Russia began to use, among other things, the services of foreign PR agencies. One of the most famous examples in this area was the American company Ketchum. An important milestone in the company's activities in Russia was the preparations for the G8 summit in St. Petersburg in 2006. Ketchum continues to interact with Russia, where its representatives work.[38]

Notes

1 All-Union Society for Cultural Relations with Abroad (VOKS). Russian Center for Science and Culture in Prague. Representative office of Rossotrudnichestvo in

the Czech Republic (in Russian). Retrieved from http://rsvk.cz/blog/2015/09/08/vsesoyuznoe-obshhestvo-kulturnoj-svyazi-s-zagranitsej-voks/

2. Russian Association for International Cooperation (RAMS) website (in Russian). Retrieved from http://rams-international.ru/
3. Later, Rossotrudnichestvo was formed on its basis.
4. Polozheniye o Rossiyskoy tsentre mezhdunarodnogo nauchnogo i kul'turnogo sotrudnichestva pri pravitel'stve Rossiyskoy Federatsii (in Russian). Retrieved from http://docs.cntd.ru/document/9008866
5. Federation B. Yeltsin of December 22, 1993 No. 2258 "On the establishment of the holding company "Russian State Television and Radio Engineering Center "Efir" and "Russian State Radio Broadcasting Company" Voice of Russia". (in Russian). Retrieved from www.innovbusiness.ru/pravo/DocumShow_DocumID_65277.html
6. Teper' ikh slyshat tol'ko nebesa. Proshchal'nyy vzglyad na radiostantsiyu "Golos Rossii". Lenta.ru. 2013, December 18. (in Russian). Retrieved from https://lenta.ru/articles/2013/12/18/voiceofrussia/
7. Concept of Foreign Policy of the Russian Federation 2000 (in Russian). Retrieved from http://docs.cntd.ru/document/901764263
8. Concept of Foreign Policy of the Russian Federation 2008 (in Russian). Retrieved from www.kremlin.ru/acts/news/785
9. Ukaz "O Rossiyskom tsentre mezhdunarodnogo nauchnogo i kul'turnogo sotrudnichestva pri Ministerstve inostrannykhdel Rossiyskoy Federatsii" (in Russian). Retrieved from www.mid.ru/web/guest/foreign_policy/official_documents/-/asset_publisher/CptICkB6BZ29/content/id/224550
10. Concept of the Foreign Policy of the Russian Federation. Approved by President of the Russian Federation V. Putin on February 12, 2013. Retrieved from www.mid.ru/search?p_p_id=3&p_p_lifecycle=0&p_p_state=maximized&p_p_mode=view&_3_struts_action=%2Fsearch%2Fsearch#
11. Foreign Policy Concept of the Russian Federation. Approved by President of the Russian Federation Vladimir Putin on November 30, 2016. Retrieved from www.mid.ru/foreign_policy/news/-/asset_publisher/cKNonkJE02Bw/content/id/2542248?p_p_id=101_INSTANCE_cKNonkJE02Bw&_101_INSTANCE_cKNonkJE02Bw_languageId=en_GB
12. Ibid.
13. Concept of the Foreign Policy of the Russian Federation. Approved by President of the Russian Federation V. Putin on February 12, 2013. Retrieved from www.mid.ru/search?p_p_id=3&p_p_lifecycle=0&p_p_state=maximized&p_p_mode=view&_3_struts_action=%2Fsearch%2Fsearch#
14. Foreign Policy Concept of the Russian Federation. Approved by President of the Russian Federation Vladimir Putin on November 30, 2016. Retrieved from www.mid.ru/en/foreign_policy/official_documents/-/asset_publisher/CptICkB6BZ29/content/id/2542248
15. Decree "On the Russian Center for International Scientific and Cultural Cooperation under the Ministry of Foreign Affairs of the Russian Federation".
16. Ibid.
17. Rossotrudnichestvo website. Retrieved from http://rs.gov.ru/en
18. Report on the results of the activities of Rossotrudnichestvo in the implementation of the powers vested in it for 2018.
19. Ukaz "O nekotorykh merakh po povysheniyu effektivnosti deyatel'nosti gosudarstvennykh sredstv massovoy informatsii" (in Russian). 2013, December 9. Retrieved from http://kremlin.ru/events/president/news/19805

20 Badanin, R. Zachem nam agentstvo "Rossiya segodnya" (in Russian). *Forbes*. Retrieved from www.forbes.ru/mneniya-column/vertikal/248408-zachem-nam-agentstvo-rossiya-segodnya
21 Margarita Simon'yan – o RIA "Novosti" i bitve za Ukrainu. Moskovskiy komsomolets. 2014, March 6 (in Russian). Retrieved from www.mk.ru/social/interview/2014/03/06/995044-margarita-simonyan-o-ria-novosti-i-bitve-za-ukrainu.html
22 Rasporyazheniye Prezidenta Rossiyskoy Federatsii ot 02.02.2010 g. № 60-rp (in Russian). Retrieved from www.kremlin.ru/acts/bank/30577
23 Aleksander Gorchakov Public Diplomacy Fund. Retrieved from https://gorchakovfund.ru/en/
24 Ukaz Prezidenta Rossiyskoy Federatsii o sozdanii fonda "Russkiy mir" (in Russian). Retrieved from www.kremlin.ru/acts/bank/25689
25 Russkiymir website. Retrieved from https://russkiymir.ru/en/
26 Poslaniye Prezidenta Rossii V. Putina Federal'nomu Sobraniyu Rossiyskoy Federatsii 26 aprelya 2007 g (in Russian). Retrieved from www.kremlin.ru/acts/bank/25522
27 See, for example, the MGIMO master's program in sports diplomacy. Retrieved from https://sports.mgimo.ru/en
28 Federal'nyy zakon o gosudarstvennoy politike Rossiyskoy Federatsii v otnoshenii sootechestvennikov za rubezhom (in Russian). Retrieved from www.consultant.ru/cons/cgi/online.cgi?req=doc&base=LAW&n=150465&fld=134&dst=100182,0&rnd=0.8636964689926614#09190351209401864
29 Chepurin, A. V. Za predelami Rossii seychas prozhivayet okolo 30 millionov nashikh sootechestvennikov. Interv'yu. 2010, April 12 g (in Russian). *Interfaks*. Retrieved from www.interfax.ru/interview/131938
30 Ukaz Prezidenta RF ot 25 maya 2011 g. N 678 "O sozdanii Fonda podderzhki i zashchity prav sootechestvennikov, prozhivayushchikh za rubezhom" (In Russian). Retrieved from https://base.garant.ru/12186106/
31 Foundation for the Support and Protection of the Rights of Compatriots Living Abroad website (in Russian). Retrieved from http://pravfond.ru/?module=pages&action=view&id=1
32 RUDN University website. Retrieved from http://eng.rudn.ru/
33 Kontseptsiya eksporta obrazovatel'nykh uslug Rossiyskoy Federatsii na period 2011 2020 gg (in Russian). Retrieved from http://vi.russia.edu.ru/news/discus/concept/3783
34 Strategiya24. Natsional'nyy proyekt "Obrazovaniye" (in Russian). Retrieved from https://strategy24.ru/rf/education/projects/natsionalnyy-proekt-obrazovanie
35 UNESCO. *Education*. Retrieved from http://data.uis.unesco.org/index.aspx?queryid=169#
36 RIA Novosti news agency (in Russian). Retrieved from https://na.ria.ru/20190514/1553468787.html
37 Trianon Dialogue website (in French). Retrieved from https://dialogue-trianon.fr/
38 Ketchum Moscow website. Retrieved from www.ketchum.com/moscow/

4 Russian studies of public diplomacy in the 2000s

The intensification of practical activities in the field of public diplomacy in Russia has led to an increase in scientific publications in this area. Public diplomacy has become one of the topics discussed in Russian international studies in scientific articles and monographs, as well as in educational literature [see, e.g., Kubyshkin & Tsvetkova, 2013]. Studies on public diplomacy are conducted not only in Moscow and St. Petersburg, but also in many other cities of Russia, in particular in Vladivostok, Nizhny Novgorod, Yekaterinburg, Irkutsk, and other cities.

There are three large groups in Russian studies of public diplomacy. The first group of studies is related to the theoretical aspects of public diplomacy problems. The second group includes studies of public diplomacy of various states and international organizations. This is probably the most numerous group of studies. The third group includes works on various areas of modern public diplomacy.

Theoretical research of public diplomacy in Russia

Theoretical studies of public diplomacy in Russia constitute a smaller part in comparison with other issues. However, this is typical not only for Russia, but also for many other states. A number of areas are also distinguished in Russian theoretical studies of the problems of public diplomacy. First of all, the issues of the relationship between public diplomacy and soft power are discussed. In most cases, Russian scholars follow Nye [2008], and Melissen [2005, p. 5], as well as many other researchers who consider public diplomacy as a key instrument of soft power. Therefore, in theoretical terms, rather than analyzing public diplomacy as a tool of soft power, it is often the soft power itself that is analyzed. However, in the Russian academic literature, the concept of soft power has not only polysemy but also various translations, which reflects the understanding of this phenomenon: for example, soft power is translated as domination (*vlast*), flexible power (*gibkaya sila*), and others [Neymark, 2016].

Today in Russia there are many interpretations of soft power. Parshin writes that soft power is understood in Russia in two ways. According to the first understanding, soft power is an instrument or a technology, mainly communicative, which involves potentially less damage to the recipient in comparison with other ("hard") tools (technologies). The second understanding of soft power is that it is considered as the potential of influence of some actor, due to its attractiveness and one's desire to join in its values [Parshin, 2014].

However, the most common understanding of soft power in Russia until recently is any nonmilitary methods of influencing the opposite side, that is, what Parshin called an "instrument" or "technology". With this approach, economic and political coercion, as well as other types of coercion, come under the definition of soft power, which contradicts the concept of Nye. Russian researchers sometimes assume that coercion can only be military or economic. Vapler, Gronskaya, and their colleagues write that soft power is a state's ability to influence using means other than military and economic coercion [Vapler et al., 2010]. In other words, any other type of coercion, according to this approach, falls into the category of soft power.

Moreover, in some cases, economic coercion is also seen as soft power. For example, Kasyuk sees soft power in the application of the US sanctions policy against Russia. He proceeds from the premise that soft power can be treated in different ways: on the one hand, as an opportunity to establish a dialogue of mutual understanding and cooperation, and on the other, as a lever of pressure and coercion [Kasyuk, 2018, p. 53]. In other words, the specifics of soft power are simply ignored. True, such statements are still rarely found in the Russian academic literature today. However, many researchers proceed from a realistic theory and prefer not to use the concept of soft power at all.

Russian scientists who see the meaning in using the concept of soft power are trying to identify its features, as well as the difference from other means of influence, the perception of soft power by the recipient, and so on. For example, Zevelev and Troitskiy write that Russia was disappointed by the West's lack of desire for full cooperation with Russia in the late 1990s and early 2000s. This led to the minimization of Russia's susceptibility to the "soft" influence of the United States [Zevelev & Troitskiy, 2006].

It should be noted that, starting around the 2010s, Russian scientific discourse hasincreasingly included an understanding of exactly what Nye defined as soft power, that is, attractiveness [see, e.g., Panova, 2010]. But attractiveness is not always analyzed in research. It is often simply overlooked. It was shown that, depending on whether a researcher works within the framework of a realistic approach, on the one hand, or a neoliberal and constructivist approach, on the other, he or she either identifies soft power and propaganda (realistic approach) or distinguishes them (neoliberal and constructivist approach) [Lebedeva, 2017a]. Realism is focused primarily on the realization of the state's own interests, as well as manifestations of competition and rivalry in the international arena. The interests of other actors are not the focus of attention in this case, which means there is no particular need to shape attractiveness. Therefore, there is not much difference between propaganda and soft power. With this approach, the understanding of the concept is often reduced to lobbying, propaganda, and a form of information cover for interference in the internal affairs of sovereign states [Kharkevich, 2014]. Realists practically do not use the concept of soft power or understand it as any non-forceful influence. In the case of neoliberalism and constructivism, the situation is the opposite, since the interests of the other side must be taken into account in policy-making.

Russian researchers are also attempting to operationalize the concept of soft power, highlighting various components in it [Pestsov & Bobylo, 2015]. And researchers from Yekaterinburg under the leadership of Rusakova set their task, based on quantitative indicators, as determining rating indicators of soft power. For example, Russia in the early 2010s, according to the scholars, took 27th place among the 40 countries they analyzed [*Soft Power . . .*, 2014].

In theoretical terms, a rather large discussion in Russia arose regarding the concepts of "public diplomacy" ("*publichnaya diplomatiya*"), "people's diplomacy" ("*narodnaya diplomatiya*"), and "citizen's diplomacy" ("*obshchestvennaya diplomatiya*"). There is no actual difference between the last two terms. The concept of people's diplomacy was more typical for the Soviet period, and the concepts of public diplomacy and citizen's diplomacy are more often used today. However, since several approaches to understanding the essence of public diplomacy have emerged in Russian studies, there are often differences between public diplomacy on the one hand and people's diplomacy and citizen's diplomacy on the other hand, depending on the context.

The first approach is that public diplomacy is identified with the activities of nongovernmental actors and is synonymous with citizen's diplomacy, as well as people's diplomacy [see, e.g., Naumov, 2017; Fedoreyeva, 2017; Mukhametov, 2014; Evdokimov, 2011]. This approach actually reduces the analysis to the activities of NGOs in the international arena and leads to frequent ignoring of the fact that the channels of public diplomacy can be both state and non-state. In other words, the state can act directly through its official representatives or indirectly through non-state actors.

The second approach assumes a broader understanding of public diplomacy, namely, as the activity of state and non-state actors [Dolinskiy, 2012]. Zonova adheres to a similar position, saying that in Russian foreign policy vocabulary there are two terms with reference to diplomacy: public diplomacy and people's diplomacy. Zonova writes that in Russia, it is called people's diplomacy when speaking about diplomacy of NGOs [Zonova, 2012].

There is also a largely politicized understanding of the differences between public diplomacy and public diplomacy. Thus, public diplomacy is defined as a type of Western European international cooperation using various means with the aim of "implanting" a certain way of life, which coincides with the concept of propaganda. Public diplomacy in its Russian version represents the cooperation of all forces of civil society for the establishment of an internal Russian dialogue, as well as the establishment of close ties and mutual understanding with representatives of foreign governments and the foreign public [Parubochnaya & Piskunov, 2018]. However, it should be noted that this point of view is not common in Russian studies of public diplomacy.

The term people's diplomacy has been used increasingly in recent years. At the same time, the public diplomacy of Russian officials is almost out of the research focus of Russian scholars.

Another of the research topics discussed is how much public diplomacy can be identified with the brand of the state, the idea of which is being developed by Anholt [2007]. This problem is not specific to Russia. It is also widely discussed by researchers from other countries. However, the idea of a state brand is now becoming popular in Russia. In a number of Russian works, branding is understood very broadly – as creating the image of the state. Thus, Semedov and Kurbatova, based on the views of Anholt, write that the state brand includes a number of components (tourism, export, investment and migration, culture and heritage, as well as management), significantly expands the list of these components, and introduces education, science, and NGOs [Semedov & Kurbatova, 2020]. At the same time, a number of Russian researchers working in the field of international relations tend to believe that it is not necessary to transfer concepts from the field of management to international relations. One of the most important differences between creating a brand and using public diplomacy is that public diplomacy necessarily involves dialogue [Zonova, 2012; Lebedeva, 2017a]. Neymark, criticizing the idea of using the concept of national branding instead of soft power or its implementation through public diplomacy, points out that the brand is aimed at being the first among similar products on the market, while soft power and public diplomacy are important such concepts as reputation [Neymark, 2017].

This raises another problem that is almost not discussed in Russian academic literature. Its essence is whether all actions in the international arena that meet the signs of soft power can be considered as public diplomacy. This question arises especially clearly in the economic sphere. If, regarding the formation of national branding, most Russian researchers in the field of international relations agree that it should not replace the concept of public diplomacy (or, at least, these two concepts require a clear distinction), then with economic (or business) diplomacy and economic cooperation, as well as development diplomacy, the situation is more complicated. Nye noted that non-state actors have soft power [2004b]. Business is no exception. Permyakova and Skryagina indicate that social responsibility is a soft power of multinational corporations [2013]. Based on the presence of soft power in business structures, a number of researchers conclude that business structures are included in public diplomacy. Thus, Tkachenko believes that development diplomacy is part of public diplomacy, since it implements its goals by using soft power resources, primarily economic, financial, and intellectual [Tkachenko, 2020]. Velikaya defines the economic direction of Russian public diplomacy as "creating conditions for attracting foreign investors and promoting Russian brands abroad" [2019, p. 502]. However, this definition "loses" the political component of public diplomacy. At the same time, an important condition for the economic direction of public policy is the implementation of the political goals of the state by business structures. Therefore, a more precise formulation was proposed by Bykov and Solntsev, who define the essence of business diplomacy as "a tool for achieving diplomatic results not through diplomatic means, but through execution of commercial agreements" [2020, p. 185], although the line here is very thin. In general, Russian business diplomacy as part of public diplomacy is to meet the criterion, which requires focus on the implementation of Russia's foreign policy goals.

The next area of research is not related to the definition of public diplomacy and people's diplomacy or to issues of national branding but to how independent non-state actors are implementing their actions in the international arena. It seems that non-state actors are in many cases quite independent and can themselves form the soft power of the country, as well as their own. Otherwise, they wouldn't be actors. At the same time, the state can provide them with direct assistance, or it can distance itself from them, and vice versa. They can assist the state in implementing soft power.

Another aspect is related to the goals of public diplomacy: is public diplomacy a means of realizing the goals of the state through non-state actors, or the goal of public diplomacy is to strengthen mutual understanding between the peoples of different states [Lukin 2013]. Apparently, both models are realized in reality. The state influences the societies of other countries through non-state structures. But interaction, mutual understanding, and dialogue between societies of different states is also carried out through public diplomacy.

Finally, one more area of research on public diplomacy in Russia can stand out. It is not widespread, and the first studies are just beginning. The essence of this area is to identify the side effects of public diplomacy and soft power that are negative, but not initially obvious. The important point here is that some side effects were not predicted when using public diplomacy. And this distinguishes this area from a large number of works in which, in fact, public diplomacy is replaced by propaganda, and criticism of its use is given. Within the framework of this newly emerging direction in Russian studies, it is noted that in order to avoid negative consequences in the use of the instrument of public diplomacy, it is necessary to form not only some positive features of the state, but also its integral image. In addition, it is important to foresee possible negative side effects of the use of soft power and public diplomacy [Lebedeva, Rustamova, & Sharko 2016]. It should be emphasized that this is not about the deliberate use of public diplomacy with negative consequences for the state in relation to which it is applied (i.e., some kind of sharp power), but about the side effects of creating an attractive image, which was not calculated in advance. For example, the creation of a positive image by the state in order to attract migrants can have a negative effect if they flow in too much.

Russian studies of public diplomacy of various states and international organizations

Russian researchers publish numerous works that study the approaches, institutions, and mechanisms of the public diplomacy of various states.

First, the public diplomacy of Russia is analyzed. Burlinova, Ivanchenko, and Gribkova [2018] point to the following areas of public diplomacy, although it is noted that not all of them are equally implemented by Russia:

- Working with compatriots
- Public diplomacy to support the historical truth and countering falsification of history in the international public space
- International youth cooperation
- Parliamentary diplomacy
- State-supported NGOs and funds in the sphere of public diplomacy
- The Russian phenomenon of Facebook and Twitter diplomacy
- Formats of cultural and language diplomacy abroad

Sports, youth, science, education, and a number of other areas should be added to the list. As for the policy of preserving historical truth and the policy of countering falsification of history in the international public space, it is undoubtedly present in the policy of the Russian Federation. However, the question is how much is implemented by means of public diplomacy.

In practical terms, Russia's public diplomacy is largely represented by cultural diplomacy, the development of twinning ties, and humanitarian cooperation [Velikaya, 2019]. The issues related to compatriots are still the least studied, although they are currently receiving a lot of attention from various practically oriented state and non-state organizations, in particular Rossotrudnichestvo.

A relatively new area in Russia is Russian public diplomacy in international organizations. The research by Chepurina and Kuznetsov focuses on Russia's public diplomacy in international organizations, in particular the UN. They show that Russian citizens work in the UN Secretariat as well as in UN peacekeeping missions; however, their numbers are significantly lower than those of the United States, France, and Great Britain. The authors note that even Canada, whose financial contribution is comparable to Russia's, has twice as many UN staff as Russia has. One of the problems with this situation is that working in the UN requires experience in working in intergovernmental organizations or NGOs. Chepurina and Kuznetsov see a solution to the problem, in particular in the development of the activities of Russian NGOs and, in general, in the more active participation of Russian people in NGOs [Chepurina & Kuznetsov, 2020]. The peculiarity of this research is that Chepurina has worked for a long time in the structures of international organizations. Therefore, the included observation method is used to a certain extent in the study.

Since one of the most important channels for implementing public diplomacy is primarily through NGOs, they are also the focus of Russian researchers. Russian NGOs developed after the disintegration of the Soviet Union. Despite the fact that a significant number of active NGOs working in the field of public diplomacy are government organized (or operated), a number of Russian NGOs operate largely independently. E. Stetsko, a researcher from St. Petersburg, sees a direct link between public diplomacy carried out by NGOs and the development of civil society in Russia. E. Stetsko proceeds proceeds from the fact that the activities of NGOs will be more effective in the conditions of active civil society [Stetsko, 2020]. Currently, only a few Russian NGOs operate abroad, providing humanitarian and medical assistance and participating in small development projects. Chepurina and Kuznetsov write, "only 281 Russian NGOs have a consultative status with The United Nations Economic and Social Council (ECOSOC) compared to the 409 NGOs from Belgium, 866 from France, and 1057 from Brazil" [Chepurina & Kuznetsov, 2020: 175].

The academic literature also deals with other issues of Russian public diplomacy, in particular those related to the problem of its organization in the country. One such question is how well public diplomacy should be coordinated. Thus, Dolinskiy believes that Russia should have a center for coordinating the public diplomacy activities of different actors [D2013a]. Burlinova and her colleagues hold a similar position. They write that in the Russian context, public diplomacy is not perceived as a system of institutions but is defined as one of the areas of work along with cultural and humanitarian cooperation, public diplomacy, and strategic communications. The key problem of Russian public diplomacy is the lack of system and coordination in the work of various departments and organizations. In Russia, all interaction between the Foreign Ministry and the public sector is limited to the activities of a single department (Department for Relations with the Subjects of the Federation, Parliament and Public Organizations), and active work with the local public in the host countries is carried out if there is a desire and activity of responsible diplomats [Burlinova, Vasilenko, Ivanchenko, & Shakirov, 2020].

Burlinova identifies eight problems in the organization of Russian public diplomacy. The first problem is the lack of system and coordination in the work of various departments and organizations due to the spontaneity of the development of public diplomacy in Russia. The second problem is that officials do not understand the essence of public diplomacy and how it should work. The third is the lack of a systemic vision of work in the field of soft power. Burlinova believes that a legally binding document should be developed indicating the basic rules of behavior, actors, and their interaction. The fourth is the problem of funding, primarily related to the lack of grants. The fifth is peculiarities of Russian NGOs, which, in her opinion, like the Russian bureaucracy, were not ready to work in the field of public diplomacy and do not understand its essence. As a continuation of this, a sixth problem is the lack of targeted training in the field of public diplomacy. The seventh is that almost no foreign NGOs are involved in Russian public diplomacy. Finally, the eighth problem is the need at the state level to change the attitude toward public diplomacy [Burlinova, 2014].

These examples show a clear desire to centralize Russian public diplomacy. How much this can be done, and most importantly how effective the centralization would be, remains in question. So, there is another point of view. Since modern relations, including in the field of public diplomacy, are increasingly acquiring network formats [Grebenkina, 2017], the question arises of how much coordination of network structures is possible. Apparently, in the modern world it will be increasingly difficult to strictly regulate public diplomacy, especially because of the numerous actors involved in it who use information and communication technologies widely. This does not mean, however, that there is no need at all for some unified basis for Russian public diplomacy.

It should certainly be unified in terms of organization, funding, and defining the main directions, forms, and methods. However, such a framework should be feedback based and largely self-tuning.

Another problem, which also partly relates to the issue of the coordination, is associated with Russian public diplomacy's practice of educational exchange programs. They allow participants to gain new knowledge, competencies, and experience and to establish new connections. At the same time, as Dolinskiy notes, in Russia it is difficult to say which agency has the resources and political mandate to assess the effectiveness of educational exchange programs. Dolinskiy writes, "in general, one can state the presence of a certain gap between existing international best practices and Russian experience" [2014, p. 60].

A significant vector of Russian public diplomacy is directed to the CIS states. Accordingly, this issue is the subject of research, which analyzes the activity of Russia as an initiator of activities in the following areas: (1) cultural diplomacy; (2) youth diplomacy; (3) education; (4) sports and tourism; (5) medicine and science; and (6) cooperation in the field of information. It is noted, in particular, that various types of activity in the framework of public diplomacy involve the participation of representatives of not only capital cities, but also small localities [Borishpolets, 2017].

In the post-Soviet space, interest for Russian researchers lies, in particular, in the states of Central Asia. Central Asia is a special region for Russia. First of all, this region has long-standing ties with Russia in many areas, including economic, scientific, technical, and educational. The roots of these ties go deep into the historical period. The Russian language has spread throughout Central Asia, which provides good opportunities for using public diplomacy. Finally, the region, which is important from a geopolitical point of view and has large mineral resources, is of great interest to many countries. Russians pay more attention to the Russian language and culture, while the United States pays more attention to the use of new technologies and the European Union countries pay more attention to human rights and environmental issues [Lebedeva, 2018].

A relatively small number of comparative studies on the public diplomacy of foreign countries and the soft power of Russia and various other states are presented in Russia. Among these studies, we should mention the article by Kazarinova, which analyzes the use of soft power by the United States, the countries of the European Union, China, and India. Thus, the author notes that the United States primarily focuses on the implementation of its soft power on issues of education and popular culture, while the EU has the attractive power of its supranational structures. China focuses on culture and sports in public diplomacy, while India focuses on sports, religion, and cinema [Kazarinova, 2011].

Another study conducted by Velikaya compares Russian and US public diplomacy. The author notes that US public diplomacy in Russia uses methods and means that were typical for it in the post-Soviet space immediately after the end of the Cold War. At that time, the United States was actively involved in the formation of Russian political institutions. Today, such activity is perceived in Russia as interference in internal affairs. In turn, Russian public diplomacy in the United States is limited to domestic American issues. Russia is more interested in the implementation of public diplomacy in those countries that together with it are included in integration associations. In other words, the vectors of the direction of public diplomacy of the two countries are different [Velikaya, 2019].

Along with the "classical" aspects of public diplomacy, in recent years attention has been paid to "peripheral" issues. Tabarintseva-Romanova compares the use of culinary diplomacy in Italy and Russia. Unlike Italy, in Russia the gastronomic theme is generally outside the political and diplomatic discourse; moreover, it does not appear in the mass media [Tabarintseva-Romanova, 2020]. It is obvious that culinary diplomacy has great prospects in Russia.

The Baltic states are a difficult region for the implementation of Russian public diplomacy. On the one hand, a large number of the Russian-speaking population live in this region; on the other, these states have entered NATO and, in general, their policy is far from being pro-Russian. However, despite the tense relations with the Baltic states, in particular with Lithuania, there are groups of people in both countries who are interested in developing a constructive dialogue even in the present conditions. At the same time, as Ivanova writes, the official media channels of the two countries often form negative images of each other. In these conditions, informal communication channels within the framework of public diplomacy become valuable, which still allow for an effective dialogue [Ivanova, 2015].

A significant part of Russian research is devoted to the analysis of public diplomacy of the world's leading states. The issues of organizing and implementing public diplomacy in the United States are studied quite carefully. There are several reasons for this. First, the United States is the country where the term "public diplomacy" originated and where public diplomacy is widely studied. Second, it is obvious that the United States has the greatest influence on modern world politics, and in this sense, how this is done is undoubtedly of interest to Russia.

One of the leading Russian researchers of US public diplomacy is Tsvetkova, professor at St. Petersburg University. She distinguishes two periods in US foreign policy. In the period 2009–2012, US public diplomacy was guided by Nye's concept of soft power. The United States pursued a policy of "attracting-engaging" a foreign target audience in relation to the values and culture of the United States. The practical implementation of this approach was reflected in the development of US digital diplomacy, in various US public diplomacy programs in the Middle East, as well as in the desire of the Obama administration to establish cooperation with some states. However, in the next period, which occurred in 2013–2015, there was a change in the principles of public diplomacy. The United States began to focus on strategic communication, which, according to Tsvetkova, is associated with an aggravation of the international situation in the world. As a result, this change of principles brought US public diplomacy closer to propaganda [Tsvetkova, 2015].

In Tsvetkova's study, first, the fact that the classical definition of public diplomacy implies the influence of the state on the society of other countries is clearly traced. And this impact can be different. Second, there is no clear boundary between soft power and hard power in the implementation of public diplomacy. Third, the reorientation of public diplomacy towards strategic communication brings it closer to propaganda. It can be assumed that in conditions of aggravation of relations between states, the idea of attractiveness in interaction will fade into the background. The parties in these conditions are more oriented towards strategic communication as a means of providing quick results.

Analyzing US public diplomacy with regard to Russia, Tsvetkova also notes that there has been a shift that affects the strengthening of American activity on the Russian Internet [Tsvetkova, 2012].

Among the countries of the European Union, Russian researchers pay attention, first of all, to countries such as Germany, France, and (recently released from the EU) Great Britain. It is noted that all these countries are characterized, first, by attention to the formation of a positive image of their country abroad [see, e.g., Bezrukova, 2014], and second, by great attention to issues of culture and language [see, e.g., Lan'shina, 2015]. It is shown that, for example, France demonstrates the ability to achieve results by forming the country's international image as a peacemaker, which affirms the universal values of democracy and takes into account the traditions of each country with respect to which public diplomacy is conducted [Nagornov, 2014].

As for Germany, as noted by Kuzina, the concept of public diplomacy as well as the concept of soft power is still being introduced there with caution. Nevertheless, the main areas of German public diplomacy are culture and language promotion; science and education; economic relations; and international development [Kuzina, 2020]. At the same time, Germany has developed a unique system for implementing the policy of soft power. Russian researchers write that Germany attaches great importance to education as a tool of soft power. Antyukhova characterizes the educational component of Germany's soft power in the following way: (1) in Germany, there is a well-planned educational strategy based on the promotion of German interests in other countries and regions under the auspices of various NGOs; (2) since the beginning of the 1990s, after the accelerated education reform, which was designed to unite the eastern and western education systems of Germany, an extensive network of management and implementation of educational programs of various levels on an international scale was created in Germany; (3) Germany absolutely rightly chose the direction of spreading its influence through education. Among the key regions, Eastern Europe should be highlighted here, which since the beginning of the 1990s actively reoriented towards the West and its values; as well as Latin America, where Germany is a serious alternative to American dominance [Antyukhova, 2019].

Non-state actors, including foundations close to political parties, dominate in public diplomacy. And the main sources of financing the activities of these organizations are the federal and regional budgets, their own incomes, membership fees, and donations [Lan'shina, 2014]. An important feature of soft power and, accordingly, German public diplomacy is that, despite significant state funding, they remain nongovernmental in nature [Rustamova, 2016].

The experience of British public diplomacy is also in the focus of Russian scholars. Shelepov names the following areas of public diplomacy in the UK: culture and language promotion; cooperation in education, scientific, technical, and innovative cooperation; development of business relations; development of public diplomacy (youth exchanges, NGO activities); promotion of international development; and others. Based on the analysis, the author concludes that the combination of various areas of international cultural and humanitarian cooperation contributes to the achievement of the main goal of the soft power policy of Great Britain – ensuring influence and successful promotion of national values abroad [Shelepov, 2014].

Russian scholars pay attention to the public diplomacy of China as a state that is rapidly increasing its influence in the international arena. In Russia, China's public diplomacy is usually linked to the soft power of this state. It was noted that although the Chinese leadership pays great attention to public diplomacy, the resources for its implementation are insufficient, particularly because of the state's opaque political system [Krivokhizh, 2012]. Estimates in other Russian studies of China's public diplomacy are less critical. Usually the focus is on the strengths of Chinese public diplomacy, one of which is its mass character [Evdokimov, 2011].

Russian researchers draw attention to the fact that in the 20th century, China, like European countries, paid special attention to culture as a significant element of soft power and public diplomacy [Sveshnikov, 2001]. In addition to the culture and popularization of the Chinese language, which is largely carried out through Confucius centers located in various parts of the world, the PRC pays great attention to providing development assistance (programs in education, health, humanitarian, and economic assistance) in Africa and Latin America, that is, primarily where China has economic interests (Kazarinova, 2011).

The structures involved in China's public diplomacy and its funding sources are considered as well [see, e.g., Bodrova, 2014]. The issue of public diplomacy of the PRC is often raised at various scientific conferences in Russia.

Russian scholars analyze not only public diplomacy towards the countries of Central Asia, but also the public diplomacy of these countries themselves. Bakhriev identifies the following parameters that may be promising for implementing soft power and public diplomacy in Tajikistan. First, in his opinion, is the historical and cultural heritage of Tajikistan. Among the diversity of cultural heritage, two objects (Sarazm and Tajik National Park) are included on the UNESCO World Heritage List. Bakhriev's second parameter is the tourist attractiveness of Tajikistan. At the same time, he emphasizes that tourism is not only an item of state revenue, but also a soft power. The third parameter is international initiatives with an emphasis on water diplomacy. Bakhriev stresses that Tajikistan has some successes in the field of water diplomacy (Tajikistan's initiatives for cooperation in the region in the field of water resources) and these successes should be consolidated. Finally, the last parameter is the need to rely on the Tajik diaspora abroad [Bakhriev, 2018].

In recent years, Iran has also paid great attention to public diplomacy regarding Central Asia. Iran has a cultural and religious resource in this region. The political and ideological features of the Central Asian states to some extent limited Iran's public diplomacy in this region. However, dialogue between Iran and Central Asian states is improving [Dzhabarri Nasir, 2019].

Iran's activity in the field of public diplomacy encourages scholars in Russia to be more attentive to the public diplomacy of this state. As Bakhriev and Jabbari write, the public diplomacy of the Islamic Republic of Iran is focused on promoting the heritage of Persian culture, language, and religion as a tool for fighting against Western values. The authors note that (1) Iran has a good cultural and civilizational potential; (2) Iran positions itself as the defender of all oppressed peoples; (3) public diplomacy is becoming one of the key tools that has moved from the theoretical research plane to the level of practice, which is reflected in the establishment of the Iranian Foreign Ministry's Center for Public and Media Diplomacy; (4) public diplomacy becomes the channel through which the ideas of the Islamic revolution spread; (5) Iran attaches great importance to cultural diplomacy; (6) Iran pays great attention to the information and technical aspects of public diplomacy, multilingual channels are created, and communication with a foreign audience is carried out, including through social networks; and (7) public diplomacy occupies one of the most important places in Iran's foreign policy [Bakhriev & Jabbari, 2017].

The Middle East is one of the most difficult regions in the world, where the interests of many states intersect. For a long historical period, Russia has been involved in the Middle East's problems. The countries of the area are highly diverse; therefore, public diplomacy towards these countries is different. Nevertheless, Rossotrudnichestvo is a key actor in the region. An important role in the region is played by the Russian Orthodox Church, whose activities have a long tradition there. Finally, the Russian Humanitarian Mission is operating in the Middle East. It implements various programs related to education, medical care, and so on [Morozov & Simons, 2020].

In addition to these countries, Russian researchers analyze the public diplomacy of other states. For example, it is noted that Turkey's public diplomacy developed with the coming to power of the Justice and Development Party. However, starting in 2011, soft power politics and public diplomacy began to falter. Turkey, due to external and internal reasons, began to change its policy to a tougher one. Nevertheless, public diplomacy continues to be used in Turkish foreign policy, including with regard to Georgia. Turkey perceives Georgia as a geographically important country that acts as a corridor between Turkey and the Turkic-speaking Muslim countries of Central Asia and the South Caucasus [Aleksanyan, 2018]. Obviously, Turkey's public diplomacy is not limited only to these regions. Turkey is largely interested in spreading the idea of neo-Ottomanism and in this regard pays attention to the countries of the Middle East. Turkey widely uses cinema as a means of public diplomacy [Zubkova, 2015].

The publications of Russian authors on public diplomacy of various countries, of course, are not limited by the listed states. The public diplomacy of many other states is being studied, including that of Norway [Shikhova, 2019], Armenia, and other Eurasian Economic Union (EAEU) states. It is emphasized that of all the EAEU countries, Russia and Kazakhstan are most actively using the instrument of public diplomacy [Borishpolets, 2015].

If public diplomacy of states is a certain obvious phenomenon, the situation with international organizations, associations, and so on is more complicated. At the same time, taking into account the fact that Melissen pointed out the presence of public diplomacy in international organizations [2005], Russian researchers began to turn to the analysis of public diplomacy of various supranational structures. Studies of public diplomacy of international organizations are few in Russia. Nevertheless, a number of Russian researchers turn to the analysis of public diplomacy of various supranational structures. Most research is devoted to the use of public diplomacy by intergovernmental organizations and supranational associations, first in the post-Soviet space, and second in the largest international ones, such as NATO and the EU. It is emphasized that all supranational organizations and international organizations use public diplomacy to create the most positive and attractive image of themselves that they can. At the same time, some organizations, for example, the EU, declare public diplomacy in their official documents. For example, the idea of public diplomacy was reflected in a document of the European Commission, which states,

> public diplomacy deals with the influence of public sentiment. It seeks to promote the interests of the EU by understanding, informing and influencing. This means a clear explanation of the goals, policies and activities of the EU and promoting understanding of these goals through dialogue with individuals, groups, institutions and the media.[1]

Zonova, considering EU public diplomacy, emphasizes that the coordination between the EU member states and the EU itself is a serious problem, since it is hardly possible at present to achieve "speaking with one voice" [2017]. While Zonova focuses on the public diplomacy of the EU as a whole, Fominykh focuses on the problems of exchange programs as one of the elements of public diplomacy of the EU [2018]. At the same time, the EU's soft power is viewed as an instrument of public diplomacy [Baykov, 2014].

NATO's public diplomacy is also being studied in Russia. Russian researchers note that NATO actively uses the full range of means and methods of public diplomacy. At the same time, the policy of public diplomacy conducted by NATO is a fairly effective tool for achieving the goals set in the sphere of the bloc's foreign policy [Antyukhova, 2017]. In contrast to NATO, public diplomacy in the Collective Security Treaty Organization (CSTO) is represented only in certain areas, although CSTO has considerable potential for using public diplomacy to prevent and resolve conflicts [Nikitina, 2017].

Perhaps the EAEU may have the most interesting opportunities in terms of public diplomacy in the post-Soviet space. The high level of integration of the EAEU countries in the past, the spread of the Russian language in the territory of these states [Lebedeva, 2015b], and structural features of the EU-type construction allow the EAEU to use the principle of "unity in diversity", emphasizing the ability of member countries to build a single economic space while maintaining its specifics.

The public diplomacy of the Union State of Russia and Belarus, as noted by Borishpolets, is distinguished by a large number of initiatives aimed at increasing the attractiveness of this association. Borishpolets identifies two vectors in the public diplomacy of the Union State of Russia and Belarus that complement each other. The first vector is more correlated with the actions of officials and leaders of partner countries, and the second with the practice of non-state actors, including public organizations, business communities, academia, and the media [Borishpolets, 2017b]. However, it should be noted that studies of how effective these actions were has not been carried out. It is also difficult to determine the further development of events and research in this area.

These examples show that soft power and public diplomacy of various countries and supranational associations are studied quite intensively by Russian scholars. The experience of various countries is discussed by Russian researchers. However, it is difficult to say how well it is taken into account in shaping the strategy of public diplomacy in Russia.

Russian studies in other areas of public diplomacy

Among other areas of Russian public diplomacy, the main four should be highlighted:

- Problems of using new technologies in public diplomacy
- Issues of education and science in public diplomacy
- Cultural and sports diplomacy
- Public diplomacy of the media

In addition to these areas, Russian studies of public diplomacy cover issues of youth contacts, parliamentary diplomacy, religious diplomacy, and support for relations with compatriots.

The use of new technologies has generated many new phenomena in world politics, including in the field of public diplomacy. Social networks, websites of state and non-governmental organizations, Twitter diplomacy, and so on have expanded the audience dramatically, and the possibility of influencing a foreign audience has been identified by such terms as digital diplomacy, Web 2.0 diplomacy, e-diplomacy, and Internet diplomacy [Tsvetkova, 2011]. Often these terms are used interchangeably and represent a means of influencing foreign audiences through digital technologies. At the same time, some researchers distinguish between these terms, noting that public diplomacy is only a part of digital diplomacy. For example, Permyakova includes in digital diplomacy the accumulation and analysis of an enormous amount of information that can be used in political forecasts and strategic planning; consular activities such as processing and preparing visa documents and making direct contacts with citizens located abroad; and for embassies to gather information and communicate in case of emergency [2012]. It should be noted that, of course, not all diplomacy carried out with the help of digital technologies can be defined as public diplomacy. At the same time, public diplomacy does not necessarily need to use digital technologies, although in recent years it has increasingly resorted to digital solutions.

There is another important aspect of using digital technologies, Russian scholars pay attention to the positive and negative consequences of the use of digital technologies in public diplomacy. Thus, along with the opportunities that the Internet offers for public diplomacy, the issue of information security is being discussed. Zinov'yeva writes that states view US digital diplomacy programs as an attempt to intervene in internal affairs, which threatens to violate their state sovereignty [2013]. Information impact is considered, for example, by Podberezkin as a mean to solve problems that previously were solved by military, economic, and other means [2016]. As a result, "public diplomacy has become an integral part of network-centric hybrid warfare, in which the role of informational influence on the enemy becomes crucial" [Podberezkin & Zhukov, 2015]. With this understanding, public diplomacy is in fact identified with strategic communication. It should be noted that the concept of strategic communication, in contrast to the concepts of soft power and public diplomacy, is rarely used in Russia.

Tsvetkova highlights a number of consequences of modern digital diplomacy or Internet diplomacy. First, the explosive growth of digital technology has led to unpredictability and cyber propaganda. The emotional and mobilization components of the impact on the external audience have intensified. Second, it increases the effectiveness of public diplomacy. Third, the role of digital diplomacy has grown in the United States during the Obama administration [Tsvetkova, 2020]. Thus, in studies on the use of digital technologies in order to influence foreign audiences one way or another, two different types of influence are touched upon, which seldom differ. Digital technologies can be used in two types of impact on foreign audiences: (1) within the framework of public diplomacy (and then they must meet the criteria of public diplomacy) and (2) within the framework of the use of strategic communication and propaganda. It is clear that this distinction is not always easy to make. However, it is extremely important to understand the nature of the impact and determine what type of impact we are dealing with.

In situations of conflict or tense relations, means of tough informational influence on the opposite side are often used. As a result, there are information wars [Manoylo, 2016], hybrid wars [Panarin, 2016], and others, which are widely described in Russian scientific literature. Indeed, in the modern world, one can increasingly find this kind of activity. Moreover, almost all states use it. However, this type of influence on a foreign audience is not related to public diplomacy.

At the same time, in situations of conflict and crisis, public diplomacy is used to reduce tension, reconcile the parties, and so on. These can be educational programs for various groups of the population with the aim of mastering the skills of negotiation and other procedures for nonviolent conflict resolution, as well as seminars on finding solutions to conflict situations for people close to the political leaders of the opposing sides in the conflict [Lebedeva, 2015a].

Effective digital public diplomacy also can be used as a tool for post-conflict settlement [Zinov'yeva, 2017]. Zinov'yeva also drew attention to the fact that effective and innovative development of Russia needs new foreign projects in the digital sphere that are aimed at strengthening the soft power and the development of science, technology, and education. When implementing such projects, a state should take into account not only the threats, but also the opportunities offered by the electronic information environment. Such opportunities are provided by the already developed and promising tools of digital diplomacy, which should not remain the exclusive prerogative of the United States [Zinov'yeva, 2016]. Obviously, information and communication technologies will develop and be used both for propaganda and for public diplomacy.

At present, there is not a lot research in the field of cultural and sports diplomacy in Russia. The publications emphasize the growing role of culture in the modern world [see, e.g., Bogolyubova, 2013]. However, in general, these studies are largely descriptive, providing a chronicle of events in the cultural or sports fields. But textbooks on sports diplomacy have appeared. For example, Bogolyubova and Nikolayeva analyze the experience of Russia, the United States, China, France, and Great Britain in the field of sports diplomacy [2019].

Another positive point is that more and more studies are being published on sports and cultural diplomacy and their regional aspects, which go beyond just recording events [see, e.g., Shlapeko, 2017; Sedunov, 2017]. For example, Shlapeko considers external cross-border relations, including cultural ones, of such a Russian region as the Republic of Karelia. She notes that public diplomacy has undergone a regional shift. As a result, she concludes that against the background of complex modern relations between Russia and the EU, it is especially important to preserve the accumulated experience of international contacts between regions and use it for the development of territories [Shlapeko, 2017]. Indeed, often through culture, sports, and interaction in the fields of education and science, international contacts are maintained, which are interrupted in the political and economic spheres.

In recent years, Russian researchers have quite intensively developed services of higher education as a tool for public diplomacy. In Russia, numerous studies are published on the role of higher education in creating a positive image through public diplomacy. They note that the educational services market is becoming more and more important in the world. And this applies not only to commercial aspects, but also to political ones. Therefore, since the 2000s, Russia has been paying great attention to this issue. The research notes that Russia has great potential for soft power in the field of education. Russia strives to improve its international image by actively promoting educational services abroad and positioning itself as a leading educational center in the CIS [Lebedeva & Fort, 2009]. It is noted that the provision of educational services to foreign citizens ensures long-term relations between societies of different countries, as well as the loyalty of foreign citizens to the state in which they studied [Panova, 2011]. Torkunov analyzes the measures taken by the state in the field of higher education in order to improve the quality of Russian education and its attractiveness and shows that in the modern world, the leadership of states is determined by the presence of a high level of education and the promotion of language and culture [Torkunov, 2012].

In addition, various educational projects are considered and their effectiveness evaluated, both in Russia and abroad[see, e.g., Dolinskiy, 2014; Fominykh, 2008], and the resources that Russia uses abroad to implement educational policies are analyzed [Naumov & Volk, 2018].

At present, special attention in Russian studies is paid to the possibilities of science in the framework of public diplomacy and the search with its help for solving international problems. Scientific diplomacy has its roots in the past. Thus, the successful experience of interaction between Soviet and Western scientists in order to resolve conflicts and prevent a nuclear catastrophe was during the Cold War. Panchenko and Torkunov noted that researchers, by their nature of activity, are not concerned about the need to simplify reality.[2] Therefore, the interaction of researchers from different countries allows us to better understand a problem and outline ways to solve it. Despite the fact that in Russia in recent years there have been publications on the problems of scientific diplomacy, it is currently difficult to name examples of scientific diplomacy similar to those that occurred during the Cold War. And this seems strange at first glance, since scientific contacts have expanded in the world. Perhaps the reason is the strong ideologization and politicization of science in the modern world. In addition, Kharitonova and Prokhorenko point out that, unlike other countries, the Russian Ministry of Foreign Affairs does not have the position of a scientific adviser. There is also no national strategy for science diplomacy, and the existing foreign infrastructure for science diplomacy is not fully utilized [Kharitonova &

Prokhorenko, 2020]. In general, the experience of other countries in the field of scientific diplomacy attracts the attention of Russian researchers [see, e.g., Shestopal & Litvak, 2016].

At the same time, new formats have emerged in Russia that can be attributed to scientific diplomacy. These are forums with the invitation of leading Russian and foreign scientists, such as Primakov Readings[3] and the international Valdai Discussion Club.[4] These are public forums. They have their own advantages, but they do not provide privacy.

The expansion of scientific contacts and the inclusion in them not only of leading scientists, but also of a significantly larger number of researchers, university professors, and students and postgraduates, has led to the formation of a virtually new area of public diplomacy – academic diplomacy. It united the fields of scientific diplomacy and educational diplomacy into a single complex. The reasons for the formation of this new complex lie in the processes of globalization and integration of higher education, which have led to a sharp expansion of the circle of participants in interaction in the field of education and science. In addition, universities have become much more active. They provide platforms for various meetings and discussions, and often invite representatives of the authorities, businesses, and journalists to these events. Finally, new technologies have provided completely different opportunities for joint discussions and development of ideas [Torkunov, 2019].

A number of studies by Russian scientists are devoted to the role of the media in the implementation of public diplomacy, and the research is carried out both by specialists in the field of international relations and to an even greater extent by specialists in the field of mass communication [see, e.g., Orlova, 2003]. The activities of Russia Today (RT) are discussed especially intensively, as a rule, with positive assessments of its activities [see, e.g., Kolevatova, 2016]. It is noted that the role of the media is especially high thanks to modern information technologies, when, along with traditional media, Internet resources are used. It is important to emphasize that although we are talking about traditional media, almost all of them have websites and accounts on social networks that work in an interactive format.

The research of Russian scientists examines the interaction of the state and the media. It is noted that the state is interested in increasing the influence in the world of those media that can widely relay information that is important to the state [Zegonov, 2008].

The use of traditional media in public diplomacy in Russia (as well as in other states) turns out to be the most difficult and problematic field. The media are aimed at a mass audience, unlike, for example, educational programs or science. Even with the implementation of cultural or sports projects, the audience is much narrower. As a result, the media in all countries use different means of influence, which do not exclude propaganda and strategic communication. Moreover, the media are used in information wars. Simultaneously with these means, public diplomacy is also used, which implies the creation of attractiveness for an external audience. Since the attractiveness for different segments of the population is different, the media are perceived ambiguously. It is obvious that the use of different means of influence by the same media leads to a decrease in trust in it.

The Russian academic literature examines the involvement of the media in wars, hybrid wars, and information wars [see, e.g., Frolova & Frolova, 2018]. The media act here as the most sensitive link, since they are oriented towards mass involvement.

In Russia, the first studies on the problems of compatriots, which were previously absent, appeared. For example, Chepurin notes that the views on the problem of compatriots have been significantly revised. In the past, the problems of compatriots were not the focus of attention. At present, it is understood that compatriots belong to a common civilizational space with Russia. Chepurin emphasizes that a strong diaspora integrated into the society of the country of residence is important for modern Russia. Meanwhile, the community of compatriots living abroad is poorly structured [Chepurin, 2009].

Russian studies on cultural diplomacy began to be published more actively. Thus, the article by Tabarintseva-Romanov is devoted to identifying the tools, mechanisms, and resources of cultural diplomacy, noting that these are effective tools for establishing a dialogue. At the same time, she controversially states that, unlike past policy, modern cultural policy is no longer associated with propaganda [Tabarintseva-Romanova, 2019].

In addition, in contrast to the Soviet period, religious diplomacy began to develop [see, e.g., Kasatkin, 2010]. Youth diplomacy and parliamentary diplomacy began to acquire great importance in Russia [see, e.g., Kon'kov & Chukov, 2019]. In general, there are a few conceptual works on these areas, as well as on the youth aspects of public diplomacy.

Notes

1 European Commission. (2007). A glance at EU public diplomacy at work: The EU's 50th anniversary celebrations around the world (p. 12). Luxembourg: Office for Official Publications of the European Communities.
2 Panchenko, V., & Torkunov, A. V. (2017, June 26). Uchenyy kak diplomat. *Rossiyskaya gazeta*. Retrieved from https://rg.ru/2017/06/26/kak-nauchnoe-sotrud nichestvo-pomogaet-resheniiu-mezhdunarodnyh-problem.html [Panchenko,

V., & Torkunov, A. V. (2017, June 26). Scientist as a diplomat. *Russian Newspaper*. Retrieved from https://rg.ru/2017/06/26/kak-nauchnoe-sotrudnichestvo-pomogaet-resheniiu-mezhdunarodnyh-problem.html]. (In Russian).
3 Primakov Readings website. Retrieved from www.primakovreadings.com/en
4 The Valdai Discussion Club website. Retrieved from https://valdaiclub.com/about/valdai/

5 Conclusion

Public diplomacy is becoming an essential tool of influence in the modern world. At the same time, the widespread understanding of public diplomacy as an instrument of state influence on foreign society requires clarification. At the end of the 20th and the beginning of the 21st centuries, a cardinal transformation of the political organization of the world has taken place. In connection with the transformation of the political organization of the world, from the point of view of public diplomacy, two points turn out to be significant. First is the massive activity of non-state actors in the international arena in the context of modern information and communication technologies. This entails the active use of a variety of information and different means for different categories of people. Second, the process of building configurations of interstate relations after the collapse of the bipolar system gave rise to a struggle for leadership between states, which led to the strengthening of various means of influencing the external audience. Public diplomacy is just one of the tools of such influence (along with propaganda, strategic communication, and the formation of national branding), the most important characteristic of which is attractiveness, that is, orientation towards soft power when using it. In addition, important criteria that distinguish public diplomacy from other types of influence are orientation towards dialogue with a foreign audience and cooperation with foreign states; openness in relationships; orientation to the foreign policy of a state that implements public diplomacy; and, in theoretical terms, the use of the concept of soft power and research within the framework of the neoliberal or constructivist paradigm. Ignoring these specific characteristics of public diplomacy leads to its identification with other means of influencing a foreign audience, and, as a consequence, to an increase in confrontation in the world.

During the Cold War era, structures and institutions began to be created to influence the audience of foreign countries, including the Soviet Union.

Conclusion

As in other states, they were focused on the implementation of public diplomacy according to the G2P formula and included the media (broadcasting), cultural, sports diplomacy, and so on. In general, the public diplomacy of the Soviet period was extremely centralized. Of particular note is the effectiveness of scientific diplomacy during the Cold War, which contributed to the conclusion of a number of agreements on disarmament issues.

After a period of decline in interest in public diplomacy in the world and in Russia in the 1990s, its revival took place in the 2000s. Russia, like a number of other countries, has turned to an instrument of public diplomacy, which has become an important part of its foreign policy. This is due to both the revival of public diplomacy in the world as a whole and the foreign policy goals of Russia. Russian interest in public diplomacy at the official level is reflected in the adoption of strategic documents, as well as in the development of public diplomacy practice. Some areas in which public diplomacy was used during the Cold War (media, cultural, scientific, and sports diplomacy) continue to be used nowadays. At the same time, new tools of public diplomacy have emerged. Thus, Internet technologies, including Web 2.0 technologies, have become an integral part of Russia's public diplomacy. In addition, the number of Russian participants in public diplomacy has increased dramatically, both in terms of their total number and in terms of the diversity of groups that have become involved in public diplomacy. This has led to the fact that Russia's public diplomacy, despite the creation of a number of new state structures, has become less centralized in comparison with the Soviet time.

The development of the practice has led to an increase in research on public diplomacy in Russia. In Russian studies of public diplomacy, several areas are highlighted. Most of the research focuses on the analysis of public diplomacy of various states, which is carried out mainly through non-state structures or actors affiliated with the state. Therefore, it is no coincidence that public diplomacy in Russia is understood as people's diplomacy or citizen's diplomacy. The approaches of various states to public diplomacy, directions, and tools are analyzed in Russia. Particular attention is paid to Russian public diplomacy. Its strengths and weaknesses are identified. There is no single point of view regarding the shortcomings of Russian public diplomacy, although a number of researchers indicate the need for its greater centralization and coordination. At the same time, the question arises here as to what extent it is possible to do this, since many actors operate in the modern world.

In addition, Russian researchers focus on such areas of public diplomacy as the role of information and communication technologies, public diplomacy in conflict and crisis relations, academic diplomacy, the role of the media, and others.

Most Russian researchers proceed from the understanding that public diplomacy is oriented toward soft power and is more open in contrast to propaganda. However, the understanding of soft power differs among various researchers. Although more and more Russian scholars now consider soft power as creating attractiveness, some researchers understand soft power only as the use of nonviolent means. In general, public diplomacy and soft power are understood uncertainly in Russia.

The relationship between public diplomacy, people's diplomacy, and citizen's diplomacy is also discussed. In other words, the question of whether public diplomacy is implemented only by non-state actors is debated. Most researchers see two channels for the implementation of public diplomacy; however, research on the official channels of public diplomacy is almost never done. Russian scientists in most cases focus on non-state actors. This raises the question of how independent non-state actors are.

An area of research is also outlined to identify the three sides of public diplomacy, which were not initially obvious.

References

Acharya, A. (2016). Advancing global IR: Challenges, contentions, and contributions. *International Studies Review, 18*, 4–15.
Achkasova, V. A., & Kostritskaya, T. B. (2004). "Russkiy mir" i problemy realizatsii proyekta Yevraziyskogo soyuza. *Yevraziyskaya integratsiya: ekonomika, pravo, politika, 1*, 117–123 [Achkasova, V. A., & Kostritskaya, T. B. (2004). "Russian World" and the problems of implementing the project of the Eurasian Union. *Eurasian Integration: Economics, Law, Politics, 1*, 117–123]. (In Russian).
Aleksanyan, L. M. (2018). Rol' publichnoy diplomatii vo vneshney politike Turtsii v otnoshenii Gruzii. *Problemy postsovetskogo prostranstva, 5*(4), 418–428. Retrieved from https://doi.org/10.24975/2313-8920-2018-5-4-418-428 [Aleksanyan, L. M. (2018). The role of public diplomacy in Turkish foreign policy towards Georgia. *Issues of the Post-Soviet Space, 5*(4), 418–428. Retrieved from https://doi.org/10.24975/2313-8920-2018-5-4-418-428]. (In Russian).
Anholt, S. (2006). Public diplomacy and place branding: Where's the link? *Place Branding, 2*, 271–275. doi:10.1057/palgrave.pb.6000040. Retrieved from https://link.springer.com/content/pdf/10.1057%2Fpalgrave.pb.6000040.pdf
Anholt, S. (2007). *Competitive identity: The new brand management for nations, regions and cities*. Palgrave Macmillan.
Antyukhova, Ye A. (2017). Nekotoryye aspekty publichnoy diplomatii NATO v usloviyakh depolyarizatsii politicheskoy sistemy mira. In M. M. Lebedeva (red.), *Publichnaya diplomatiya: Teoriya i praktika* (S. 128–143). Moskva: Aspekt Press [Antyuhova, E. A. (2017). Some aspects of NATO's public diplomacy in conditions of depolarization of the political system of the world. In M. M. Lebedeva (Ed.), *Public diplomacy: Theory and practice* (pp. 128–143). Moscow: Aspect Press]. (In Russian).
Antyukhova, Ye A. (2019). Obrazovaniye kak instrument "myagkoy sily" vo vneshney politike Germanii. *Vestnik Tomskogo gosudarstvennogo universiteta. Istoriya, 57*, 41–45. doi:10.17223/19988613/57/6. Retrieved from www.elibrary.ru/download/elibrary_37182456_55347115.pdf [Antyuhova, E. A. (2019). Education as a tool of soft power in German foreign policy. *Bulletin of Tomsk State University. History, 57*, 41–45. doi:10.17223/19988613/57/6. Retrieved from www.elibrary.ru/download/elibrary_37182456_55347115.pdf]. (In Russian).

References

Bakhriev, B. Kh. (2018). "Myagkaya sila" i publichnaya diplomatiya: vozmozhnosti dlya nezavisimogo Tadzhikistana. *Vestnik Tomskogo gosudarstvennogo universiteta, 436*, 97–105. Retrieved from https://tsuvestnik.elpub.ru/jour/article/view/1260 [Bakhriev, B. Kh. (2018). Soft power and public diplomacy: Opportunities for independent Tajikistan. *Bulletin of Tomsk State University, 436*, 97–105]. Retrieved from https://tsuvestnik.elpub.ru/jour/article/view/1260]. (In Russian).

Bakhriev, B. Kh, & Dzhabbari, Kh R. (2017). Publichnaya diplomatiya vo vneshney politike Islamskoy Respubliki Iran. In M. M. Lebedeva (red.), *Publichnaya diplomatiya: Teoriya i praktika* (S. 194–216). Moskva: Aspekt Press [Bakhriev, B. H., & Jabbari, H. R. (2017). Public diplomacy in the foreign policy of the Islamic Republic of Iran. In M. M. Lebedeva (Ed.), *Public diplomacy: Theory and practice* (pp. 194–216). Moscow: Aspect Press]. (In Russian).

Baykov, A. A. (2014). "Myagkaya moshch'" Yevropeyskogo Soyuza v global'nom silovom ravnovesii: yevro-rossiyskiy trek. *Vestnik MGIMO-Universiteta, 2*(35), 36–46. Retrieved from https://vestnik.mgimo.ru/jour/article/view/61/61 [Baykov, A. A. (2014). Soft power of the European Union in the global power balance: Euro-Russian track. *MGIMO Review of International Relations, 2*(35), 36–46]. Retrieved from https://vestnik.mgimo.ru/jour/article/view/61/61]. (In Russian).

Bezrukova, M. (2014). Osobennosti obshchestvennoy diplomatii Germanii v Rossii. *Trendy i upravleniye, 3*, 237–242. doi:10.7256/2454-0730.2014.3.12726. Retrieved from https://nbpublish.com/library_read_article.php?id=12726 [Bezrukova, M. (2014). Features of German public diplomacy in Russia. *Trends and Management, 3*, 237–242. doi:10.7256/2454-0730.2014.3.12726. Retrieved from https://nbpublish.com/library_read_article.php?id=12726]. (In Russian).

Bodrova, O. I. (2014). Rol' "Narodnoy diplomatii" v komplekse diplomaticheskogo instrumentariya KNR. *Vestnik Nizhegorodskogo universiteta im. N. I. Lobachevskogo, 5*, 64–68 [Bodrova, O. I. (2014). The role of "people's diplomacy" in the complex of diplomatic tools of the PRC. *Bulletin of the Nizhny Novgorod University. N.I. Lobachevsky, 5*, 64–68]. (In Russian).

Bogolyubova, N. M. (2013). Vneshnyaya kul'turnaya politika Rossii: istoricheskiy opyt i problemy sovremennogo perioda. *Vestnik Sankt-Peterburgskogo universiteta. Seriya 6, 3*, 143–146 [Bogolyubova, N. M. (2013). Foreign cultural policy of Russia: Historical experience and problems of the current period. *Bulletin of St. Petersburg University. Series 6, 3*, 143–146]. (In Russian).

Bogolyubova, N. M., & Nikolayeva, Yu V. (2019). *Geopolitika sporta i osnovy sportivnoy diplomatii*. Moskva: Izdatel'stvo Yurayt [Bogolyubova, N. M., & Nikolaeva, Yu V. (2019). *Geopolitics of sport and the basics of sports diplomacy*. Moscow: Yurayt Publishing House]. (In Russian).

Borishpolets, K. P. (2015). Publichnaya diplomatiya na prostranstve YEAES: osmysleniye fenomena i tendentsiy razvitiya. *Vestnik MGIMO-Universiteta, 5*(44), 42–49. Retrieved from https://vestnik.mgimo.ru/jour/article/view/418/418 [Borishpolets, K. P. (2015). Public diplomacy in the EAEU: An understanding of the phenomenon and tendencies of development. *MGIMO Review of International Relations, 5*(44), 42–49]. Retrieved from https://vestnik.mgimo.ru/jour/article/view/418/418]. (In Russian).

References

Borishpolets, K. P. (2017). Publichnaya diplomatiya SNG: vklad v razvitiye regional'nogo integratsionnogo sotrudnichestva i preodoleniya konfliktnykh vyzovov. In M. M. Lebedeva (red.), *Publichnaya diplomatiya: Teoriya i praktika* (S. 89–111). Moskva: Aspekt Press [Borishpolets, K. P. (2017). CIS public diplomacy: A contribution to the development of regional integration cooperation and overcoming conflict challenges. In M. M. Lebedeva (Ed.), *Public diplomacy: Theory and practice* (pp. 89–111). Moscow: Aspect Press]. (In Russian).

Burlinova, N. V. (2014). Publichnaya diplomatiya Rossii: praktika i problemy stanovleniya. *Vestnik Analitiki*, 3(57), 28–35. Retrieved from www.isoa.ru/docs/vestnik_2014-357.pdf [Burlinova, N. V. (2014). Public diplomacy of Russia: Practice and problems of formation. *Bulletin of Analytics*, 3(57), 28–35. Retrieved from www.isoa.ru/docs/vestnik_2014-357.pdf]. (In Russian).

Burlinova, N. V., Ivanchenko, V., & Gribkova, D. (2018). *Rossiyskaya publichnaya diplomatiya v 2017 godu. Obzor osnovnykh sobytiy i trendov*. Moskva: "Tsentr podderzhki i razvitiya obshchestvennykh initsiativ – Kreativnaya diplomatiya" [Burlinova, N., Ivanchenko, V., & Gribkova, D. (2018). *Russian public diplomacy in 2017. Overview of key events and trends*. Moscow: "Center for Support and Development of Public Initiatives – Creative Diplomacy"]. (In Russian).

Burlinova, N. V., Vasilenko, P., Ivanchenko, V., & Shakirov, O. (2020). *10 shagov na puti k effektivnoy publichnoy diplomatii Rossii. Ekspertnyy obzor rossiyskoy publichnoy diplomatii v 2018–2019 gg*. No 52/2020. Sayt Rossiyskogo Soveta po mezhdunarodnym delam. Retrieved from https://russiancouncil.ru/papers/RussianPublicDiplomacy-Report52-Rus.pdf [Burlinova, N., Vasilenko, P., Ivanchenko, V., & Shakirov, O. (2020). *10 steps towards effective public diplomacy in Russia. An expert review of Russian public diplomacy in 2018–2019*. No. 52/2020. Website of the Russian Council on Foreign Affairs. Retrieved from https://russiancouncil.ru/papers/RussianPublicDiplomacy-Report52-Rus.pdf]. (In Russian).

Bykov, A., & Solntsev, K. (2020). Russian business diplomacy in Southeast Asia. Russian public diplomacy and nation branding. In A. Velikaya & G. Simons (Eds.), *Russia's public diplomacy: Evolution and practice* (pp. 183–200). Palgrave Macmillan.

Chepurin, A. (2009). "Tri kita" rossiyskoy diasporal'noy politiki. *Rossiya v global'noy politike*, 3, 127–138. Retrieved from http://globalaffairs.ru/number/n_13207 [Chepurin, A. (2009). "Three Pillars" of Russian diasporal politics. *Russia in Global Affairs*, 3, 127–138. Retrieved from http://globalaffairs.ru/number/n_13207]. (In Russian).

Chepurina, M., & Kuznetsov, E. (2020). Multiple facets of Russian public diplomacy in international organizations: A case study. In A. Velikaya & G. Simons (Eds.), *Russia's public diplomacy: Evolution and practice* (pp. 167–181). Palgrave Macmillan.

Cull, N. J. (2009). *Public diplomacy: Lessons from the past*. Los Angeles: Figueroa Press. Retrieved from www.uscpublicdiplomacy.org/sites/uscpublicdiplomacy.org/files/useruploads/u35361/2009%20Paper%202.pdf

Dictionary of International Relations Terms. (1987). U.S. Department of State Library (3rd ed., pp. 85–86). Retrieved from https://books.google.ru/books?id=

References

XfWOAAAAMAAJ&pg=PA83&hl=ru&source=gbs_toc_r&cad=2#v=onepage &q&f=false

Dolinskiy, A. (2011a). Diskurs o publichnoy diplomatii. *Mezhdunarodnyye protsessy*, *1*(25), 63–73. Retrieved from www.intertrends.ru/old/twenty-fifth/008.htm [Dolinsky, A. (2011). Discourse on public diplomacy. *International Processes*, *1*(25), 63–73. Retrieved from www.intertrends.ru/old/twenty-fifth/008.htm]. (In Russian).

Dolinskiy, A. (2011b). Evolyutsiya teoreticheskikh osnovaniy publichnoy diplomatii. Evolyutsiya teoreticheskikh osnovaniy publichnoy diplomatii. *Vestnik MGIMO Universiteta*, *2*(17), 275–280 [Dolinsky, A. (2011b). Evolution of the theoretical foundations of public diplomacy. Evolution of the theoretical foundations of public diplomacy. *MGIMO Review of International Relations*, *2*(17), 275–280]. (In Russian).

Dolinskiy, A. V. (2012). Chto takoye obshchestvennaya diplomatiya i zachem ona nuzhna Rossii? *Rossiyskiy sovet po mezhdunarodnym delam*. Retrieved from http://russiancouncil.ru/analytics-and-comments/analytics/chto-takoe-obshchestvennaya-diplomatiya-i-zachem-ona-nuzhna-/ [Dolinsky, A. (2012). What is public diplomacy and why does Russia need it? *Russian Council on Foreign Affairs*. Retrieved from http://russiancouncil.ru/analytics-and-comments/analytics/chto-takoe-obshchestvennaya-diplomatiya-i-zachem-ona-nuzhna-/]. (In Russian).

Dolinskiy, A. V. (2013a, sentyabrya 26). Publichnaya diplomatiya dlya biznesa, NKO i universitetov. *Rossiyskiy Sovet po mezhdunarodnym delam.*. Retrieved from http://russiancouncil.ru/analytics-and-comments/analytics/publichnaya-diplomatiya-dlya-biznesa-nko-i-universitetov/ [Dolinsky, A. (2013, September 26). Public diplomacy for business, NGOs and universities. *Russian Council on Foreign Affairs*. Retrieved from http://russiancouncil.ru/analytics-and-comments/analytics/publichnaya-diplomatiya-dlya-biznesa-nko-i-universitetov/]. (In Russian).

Dolinskiy, A. V. (2013b, June 21). How Moscow understands soft power. *Russia Direct*. Retrieved from https://russia-direct.org/analysis/how-moscow-understands-soft-power

Dolinskiy, A. V. (2014). Obrazovatel'nyye obmeny v publichnoy diplomatii: rossiyskiy i zarubezhnyy opyt. *Vestnik MGIMO-Universiteta*, *2*(35), 56–62. Retrieved from https://vestnik.mgimo.ru/jour/article/view/63/63 [Dolinsky, A. V. (2014). Educational exchanges in public diplomacy: Russian and foreign experience. *MGIMO Review of International Relations*, *2*(35), 56–62. Retrieved from https://vestnik.mgimo.ru/jour/article/view/63/63]. (In Russian).

Dzhabarri Nasir, Kh R. (2019). Osobennosti formirovaniya tsentral'noaziatskogo napravleniya publichnoy diplomatii Irana. *Izdaniye Saratovskogo universiteta. Seriya Sotsiologiya. Politologiya*, *19*(1), 106–112. Retrieved from https://cyberleninka.ru/article/n/osobennosti-formirovaniya-tsentralnoaziatskogo-napravleniya-publichnoy-diplomatii-irana/viewer [Jabarri Nasir, H. R. (2019). Features of the formation of the Central Asian direction of public diplomacy of Iran. *Edition of the Saratov University. Series Sociology. Political Science*, *19*(1), 106–112. Retrieved from https://cyberleninka.ru/article/n/osobennosti-formirovaniya-tsentralnoaziatskogo-napravleniya-publichnoy-diplomatii-irana/viewer]. (In Russian).

Fedoreyeva, A. Yu. (2017). Publichnaya diplomatiya Kitaya. In *Nauka segodnya: vyzovy i puti ikh resheniya. Materialy mezhdunarodnoy nauchnoprakticheskoy konferentsii* (S. 144–145). Vologoda: Marker [Fedoreeva, A. Yu. (2017). Public diplomacy of China. In *Science today: Challenges and solutions. Materials of the International Scientific-Practical Conference* (pp. 144–145). Vologda: Marker]. (In Russian).

Fominykh, A. Ye. (2008). "Myagkaya moshch'" obmennykh programm. *Mezhdunarodnyye protsessy*, *6*(1), 76–85 [Fominykh, A. (2008). Soft power of exchange programs. *International Processes*, *6*(1), 76–85]. (In Russian).

Fominykh, A. Ye. (2018). *Publichnaya diplomatiya YeS. Vneshnyaya politika i mezhdunarodnyye svyazi Yevropeyskogo soyuza: Osmyslivaya rol' YeS v mire*. Irkutsk: Ottisk. Retrieved from www.volgatech.net/Jean_Monnet_centre/publication/ Irkutsk_EU%20Public%20Diplomacy%20article.pdf [Fominykh, A. E. (2018). *EU public diplomacy. European Union foreign policy and international relations: Reflecting on the EU's role in the world*. Irkutsk: Imprint. Retrieved from www.volgatech.net/Jean_Monnet_centre/publication/Irkutsk_EU%20Public%20Diplomacy%20article.pdf]. (In Russian).

Frolova, I. I., & Frolova, A. A. (2018). *Informatsionnaya voyna v sovremennykh SMI kak faktor manipulyativnogo vozdeystviya na obshchestvo: monografiya*. Kursk: Izdatel'stvo ZAO "Universitetskaya kniga" [Frolova, I. I., & Frolova, A. A. (2018). *Information warfare in modern media as a factor of manipulative influence on society: Monograph*. Kursk: Publishing house "University Book"]. (In Russian).

Fukuyama, F. (1989, Summer). The end of history? *The National Interest*, *16*, 3–18.

Gotz, N. (2011). Civil society and NGO: Far from unproblematic concepts. In B. Renalda (Ed.), *The Ashgate research companion to non-state actors* (pp. 185–196). Burlington: Ashgate.

Grebenkina, Ye. (2017). Sovremennaya diplomatiya na puti k setevoy strukture mira. *Mezhdunarodnaya zhizn'*, *4*, 99–112 [Grebenkina, E. (2017). Modern diplomacy on the way to the network structure of the world. *International Affairs*, *4*, 99–112]. (In Russian).

Gridnev, Yu A. (2000). *Sozdaniye VOKS. Zadachi i tseli. Istoriki razmyshlyayut* (Vyp. 2, S. 285–299). Moskva: Zvezdopad. Retrieved from https://rusneb.ru/ catalog/000202_000005_265324/ [Gridnev, Yu A. (2000). *Creation of VOKS. Tasks and goals. Historians ponder* (No. 2, pp. 285–299). Moscow: Zvezdopad. Retrieved from https://rusneb.ru/catalog/000202_000005_265324/]. (In Russian).

Gromoglasova, Ye S. (2018). *Gumanitarnaya diplomatiya v sovremennykh mezhdunarodnykh otnosheniyakh: opyt sistemnogo issledovaniya*. Moskva: IMEMO RAN [Gromoglasova, Ye S. (2018). *Gumanitarnaya diplomatiya v sovremennykh mezhdunarodnykh otnosheniyakh: opyt sistemnogo issledovaniya*. Moscow: IMEMO RAN]. (In Russian).

Ivanova, N.A. (2015). Ofitsial'nyy i publichnyy dialog mezhdu Litvoy i Rossiyey: poisk kommunikativnykh resheniy. *Vestnik MGIMO-Universiteta*, *5*(44), 63–71. Retrieved from https://vestnik.mgimo.ru/jour/article/view/420/420 [Ivanova, N.A. (215). Official and public dialogue in Lithuania-Russia relationships: In search of communicative solutions. *MGIMO Review of International Relations*, *5*(44), 63–71]. Retrieved from https://vestnik.mgimo.ru/jour/article/view/420/420 (In Russian).

Jowett, G., & O'Donnel, V. (2012). *Propaganda and persuasion* (5th ed.). Los Angeles and London.

Kasatkin, P. I. (2010). Russkaya pravoslavnaya tserkov' kak aktor mirovoy politiki. *Vestnik MGIMO-Universiteta*, *6*(15), 141–151 [Kasatkin, P. I. (2010). The Russian Orthodox Church as an actor in world politics. *MGIMO Review of International Relations*, *6*(15), 141–151]. (In Russian).

Kasyuk, A. Ya. (2018). "Myagkaya sila" i sanktsionnaya politika Zapada. Vestnik Moskovskogo gosudarstvennogo lingvisticheskogo universiteta. *Obshchestvennyye nauki*, *2*(800), 50–66 [Kasyuk, A. Ya. (2018). Soft power and the Western sanctions policy. Bulletin of the Moscow State Linguistic University. *Social Sciences*, *2*(800), 50–66]. (In Russian).

Kazarinova, D. (2011). Fenomen "myagkoy sily". *Svobodnaya mysl'*, *3*(1622), 187–200 [Kazarinova, D. (2011). The phenomenon of soft power. *Svobodnaya mysl*, *3*(1622), 187–200]. (In Russian).

Keohane, R. O., & Nye, J. S. (1971). Transnational relations and world politics: An introduction. *International Organization*, *25*(3), 329–349.

Kharitonova, E., & Prokhorenko, I. (2020). Russian science diplomacy. Russian public diplomacy and nation branding. In A. Velikaya & G. Simons (Eds.), *Russia's public diplomacy: Evolution and practice* (pp. 133–146). Palgrave Macmillan.

Kharkevich, M. V. (2014). "Myagkaya sila": politicheskoye ispol'zovaniye nauchnoy kontseptsii. *Vestnik MGIMO Universiteta*, *2*(35), 26–27 [Kharkevich, M. V. (2014). Soft power: The political use of a scientific concept. *MGIMO Review of International Relations*, *2*(35), 26–27]. (In Russian).

Kissinger, H. (2014). *World order*. New York: Penguin Press.

Kolevatova, T. S. (2016). Sovremennyye sredstva informatsii v publichnoy diplomatii Rossii. *Vlast*, *24*(1), 51–56 [Kolevatova, T. S. (2016). Modern media in Russian public diplomacy. *Vlast*, *24*(1), 51–56]. (In Russian).

Kon'kov, A. Ye, & Chukov, R. S. (2019). Parlamentskaya diplomatiya i kul'tura parlamentskogo dialoga v sovremennoy politike. *Gosudarstvennoye upravleniye. Elektronnyy vestnik*, 77, 124–143. doi:10.24411/2070-1381-2019-10021 [Konkov, A. E., & Chukov, R. S. (2019). Parliamentary diplomacy and the culture of parliamentary dialogue in modern politics. *Public Administration. Electronic Bulletin*, 77, 124–143. doi:10.24411/2070-1381-2019-10021]. (In Russian).

Kononenko, V. A. (2006). Sozdat' obraz Rossii? Rossij v global'noj politike. No 2 (mart–aprel'). Retrieved from www.globalaffairs.ru/number/n_6562 [Kononenko, V. A. (2006). *Create the Image of Russia? Russia in Global Politics*. No. 2 (March–April). Retrieved from www.globalaffairs.ru/number/n_6562]. (In Russian).

Kornilov, A., & Makarychev, A. (2015). *Religion, nation and democracy in the South Caucasus*. Series "Routledge contemporary Russia and Eastern Europe series" (pp. 238–254). A. Agadjanian, A. Jödicke, & E. van der Zweerde (Eds.). Routledge: London and New York.

58 References

Kovalenko, S. A., & Smolik, N. G. (2014). Uchastiye RUDN v deyatel'nosti setevogo universiteta SNG. *Vestnik RUDN. Seriya mezhdunarodnyye otnosheniya, 4,* 207–213 [Kovalenko, S. A., & Smolik, N. G. (2014). Participation of RUDN University in the activities of the CIS Network University. *RUDN Bulletin.* International Relations Series, *4,* 207–213]. (In Russian).

Krivokhizh, S.V. (2012). «Myagkaya sila» i publichnaya diplomatiya v teorii i vneshnepoliticheskoy praktike Kitaya. *Vestnik Sankt-Peterburgskogo universiteta. Seriya 13.* Vostokovedeniye. Afrikanistika, *3,* 103–111. Retrieved from https://cyberleninka.ru/article/n/myagkaya-sila-i-publichnaya-diplomatiya-v-teorii-i-vneshnepoliticheskoy-praktike-kitaya/viewer [Krivokhizh, S.V. (2012). "Soft power" and public diplomacy in theory and foreign policy practice of China. *Bulletin of St. Petersburg University. Series 13.* Oriental studies. African Studies, *3,* 103–111]. Retrieved from https://cyberleninka.ru/article/n/myagkaya-sila-i-publichnaya-diplomatiya-v-teorii-i-vneshnepoliticheskoy-praktike-kitaya/viewer (In Russian).

Kubyshkin, A. I., & Tsvetkova, N. A. (2013). *Publichnaya diplomatiya SShA.* Moskva: Aspekt Press [Kubyshkin, A. I., & Tsvetkova, N. A. (2013). *USA public diplomacy.* Moscow: Aspect Press]. (In Russian).

Kuzina, O. Ye. (2020). Diskurs publichnoy diplomatii Germanii (2014–2019 gg.). *Manuskript, 13*(5), 94–99 [Kuzina, O. E. (2020). Discourse on public diplomacy in Germany (2014–2019). *Manuscript, 13*(5), 94–99]. (In Russian).

Lan'shina, T. A. (2014). "Myagkaya sila" Germanii: kul'tura, obrazovaniye, nauka. *Vestnik mezhdunarodnykh organizatsiy: obrazovaniye, nauka, novaya ekonomika, 2,* 28–58 [Lanshina, T. A. (2014). Soft power of Germany: Culture, education, science. *International Organisations Research Journal, 2,* 28–58]. (In Russian).

Lan'shina, T. A. (2015). "Myagkaya sila" Gote-Instituta. *Vestnik mezhdunarodnykh organizatsiy: obrazovaniye, nauka, novaya ekonomika, 10*(1), 118–142 [Lanshina, T. A. (2015). The soft power of the Goethe Institute. *International Organisations Research Journal, 10*(1), 118–142]. (In Russian).

Lebedeva, M. M. (2015a). Publichnaya diplomatiya v uregulirovanii konfliktov. *Mezhdunarodnyye protsessy, 13*(4), 45–56. doi:10.17994/IT.2015.13.4.43.3. Retrieved from www.intertrends.ru/forty-third/Lebedeva.pdf [Lebedeva, M. M. (2015a). Public diplomacy in conflict resolution. *International Processes, 13*(4), 45–56. doi:10.17994/IT.2015.13.4.43.3. Retrieved from www.intertrends.ru/forty-third/Lebedeva.pdf]. (In Russian).

Lebedeva, M. M. (2015b). Sotsial'no-gumanitarnyy resurs razvitiya na yevraziyskom prostranstve. *Yevraziyskaya integratsiya: ekonomika, pravo, politika, 1*(17), 161–167 [Lebedeva, M. M. (2015b). Social and humanitarian development resource in the Eurasian space. *Eurasian Integration: Economics, Law, Politics, 1*(17), 161–167]. (In Russian).

Lebedeva, M. M. (2017a). "Myagkaya sila": ponyatiye i podkhody. *Vestnik MGIMO-Universiteta, 3*(54), 212–223. doi:10.24833/2071-8160-2017-3-54-212-223. Retrieved from www.vestnik.mgimo.ru/razdely/issledovatelskie-stati/myagkaya-sila-ponyatie-i-podhody [Lebedeva, M. M. (2017a). Soft power: Concept and approaches. *MGIMO Review of International Relations*, *3*(54), 212–223. doi:10.24833/2071-8160-2017-3-54-212-223. Retrieved from www.vestnik. mgimo.ru/razdely/issledovatelskie-stati/myagkaya-sila-ponyatie-i-podhody]. (In Russian).

Lebedeva, M. M. (2017b). Publichnaya diplomatiya: ischeznoveniye ili novyye gorizonty? In M. M. Lebedeva (red.), *Publichnaya diplomatiya: Teoriya i praktika* (S. 8–20). Moskva: Aspekt Press [Lebedeva, M. M. (2017b). Public diplomacy: Extinction or new horizons? In M. M. Lebedeva (Ed.), *Public diplomacy: Theory and practice* (pp. 8–20). Moscow: Aspect Press]. (In Russian).

Lebedeva, M. M. (2018). Razvitiye sotsial'noy i gumanitarnoy problematiki v mezhdunarodnykh issledovaniyakh: rossiyskiy rakurs. *Vestnik MGIMO – Universiteta*, *1*(58), 7–25. doi:10.24833/2071-8160-2018-1-58-7-25 [Lebedeva, M. M. (2018). The development of social and humanitarian issues in international research: A Russian perspective. *MGIMO Review of International Relations*, *1*(58), 7–25. doi:10.24833/2071-8160-2018-1-58-7-25]. (In Russian).

Lebedeva, M. M., Borishpolets, K. P., Ivanova, N. A., & Chepurina, M. A. (2016). *Tsentral'naya Aziya. Sotsial'no-gumanitarnoye izmereniye*. Moskva: Aspekt Press [Lebedeva, M. M., Borishpolets, K. P., Ivanova, N. A., & Chepurina, M. A. (2016). *Central Asia. The social and humanitarian dimension*. Moscow: Aspect Press]. (In Russian).

Lebedeva, M. M., & Fort, J. (2009). Vyssheye obrazovaniye kak potentsial "myagkoy sily" Rossii. *Vestnik MGIMO – Universiteta*, *4*, 200–205 [Lebedeva, M. M., & Fort, J. (2009). Higher education as the potential of Russia's soft power. *MGIMO Review of International Relations*, *4*, 200–205]. (In Russian).

Lebedeva, M. M., Rustamova, L. R., & Sharko, M. V. (2016). "Myagkaya sila": tyomnaya storona (na primere Germanii). *Vestnik MGIMO-Universiteta*, *3*, 144–153. Retrieved from www.vestnik.mgimo.ru/sites/default/files/pdf/013_lebedevamm_rustamovalr_sharkomv.pdf [Lebedeva, M. M., Rustamova, L. R., & Sharko, M. V. (2016). Soft power: The dark side (example of Germany). *MGIMO Review of International Relations*, *3*, 144–153. Retrieved from www.vestnik. mgimo.ru/sites/default/files/pdf/013_lebedevamm_rustamovalr_sharkomv.pdf]. (In Russian).

Leonard, M. (2002). *Public diplomacy*. London: Foreign Policy Centre. Retrieved from www.guillaumenicaise.com/wp-content/uploads/2013/10/mark-leonard_public-diplomacy.pdf

Lukin, A. V. (2013). Publichnaya diplomatiya. *Mezhdunarodnaya zhizn'*, *3*, 69–87 [Lukin, A. V. (2013). Public diplomacy. *International Affairs*, *3*, 69–87]. (In Russian).

Manoylo, A. V. (2016). Informatsionnaya voyna kak ugroza rossiyskoy natsii. *Vestnik rossiyskoy natsii*, *6*, 174–184 [Manoilo, A. V. (2016). Information war as a threat to the Russian nation. *Bulletin of the Russian Nation*, *6*, 174–184]. (In Russian).

Melissen, J. (2005). The new public diplomacy: Between theory and practice. In J. Melissen (Ed.), *The new public diplomacy: Soft power in international relations* (pp. 3–27). Houndmills, Basingstoke, Hampshire: Palgrave Macmillan. Retrieved from www.culturaldiplomacy.org/academy/pdf/research/books/soft_power/The_ New_Public_Diplomacy

Mizherikov, V. A. (2015). Detskaya "diplomatiya": istoki i perspektivy razvitiya. In L. N. Gorbunova (red.), *Konferentsium ASOU: sbornik nauchnykh trudov i materialov nauchno-prakticheskikh konferentsiy* (S. 107–111). Moskva: ASOU [Mizherikov, V. A. (2015). Children's "diplomacy": Origins and development prospects. In L. N. Gorbunova (Ed.), *ASOU conference: Collection of scientific papers and materials of scientific and practical conferences* (pp. 107–111). Moscow: ASOU]. (In Russian).

Morozov, V., & Simons, G. (2020). Russia's public diplomacy in the Middle East. Russian public diplomacy and nation branding. In A. Velikaya & G. Simons (Eds.), *Russia's public diplomacy: Evolution and practice* (pp. 233–256). Palgrave Macmillan.

Moskovskiy, M. A. (2013). Dartmutskiy dialog: pervyye shagi neformal'noy sovetsko-amerikanskoy diplomatii. *Vestnik RUDN. Seriya Mezhdunarodnyye otnosheniya*, 3, 33–47 [Moskovskiy, M. A. (2013). Dartmouth dialogue: The first steps of informal Soviet-American diplomacy. *Bulletin of the RUDN University. Series International Relations*, 3, 33–47]. (In Russian).

Mukhametov, R. S. (2014). Spetsifika obshchestvennoy diplomatii kak instrumenta vneshney politiki gosudarstva. *Izvestiya Ural'skogo federal'nogo universiteta. Seriya 3. Obshchestvennyye nauki*, 2(128), 84–90. Retrieved from http://elar.urfu.ru/bitstream/10995/25264/1/iuro-2014-128-10.pdf [Mukhametov, R. S. (2014). The specifics of public diplomacy as an instrument of state foreign policy. *Proceedings of the Ural Federal University. Series 3. Social Sciences*, 2(128), 84–90. Retrieved from http://elar.urfu.ru/bitstream/10995/25264/1/iuro-2014-128-10.pdf]. (In Russian).

Nagornov, V. A. (2014). "Myagkaya sila" po-frantsuzski. *Vestnik mezhdunarodnykh organizatsiy*, 9(2), 167–189 [Nagornov, V. A. (2014). Soft power in French. *International Organisations Research Journal*, 9(2), 167–189]. (In Russian).

Naumov, A. O. (2017). K voprosu o perspektivakh sportivnoy diplomatii Rossii (na primere populyarizatsii bor'by sambo). *Gosudarstvennoye upravleniye. Elektronnyy vestnik*, 62, 56–70. Retrieved from https://cyberleninka.ru/article/n/k-voprosu-o-perspektivah-sportivnoy-diplomatii-rossii-na-primere-populyarizatsii-borby-sambo/viewer [Naumov, A. O. (2017). On the issue of the prospects for sports diplomacy in Russia (by the example of the popularization of Sambo wrestling). *Public Administration. Electronic Bulletin*, 62, 56–70. Retrieved from https://cyberleninka.ru/article/n/k-voprosu-o-perspektivah-sportivnoy-diplomatii-rossii-na-primere-populyarizatsii-borby-sambo/viewer]. (In Russian).

Naumov, A. O., & Volk, A. Ye. (2018). Eksport rossiyskogo obrazovaniya kak instrument myagkoy sily vo vneshney politike Rossii. Gosudarstvennoye upravleniye Rossiyskoy Federatsii: vyzovy i perspektivy. In *Materialy 15-y Mezhdunarodnoy konferentsii Gosudarstvennoye upravleniye v XXI veke* (C. 558–563). Moskva: MGU [Naumov, A. O., & Volk, A. E. (2018). Export of Russian education as an instrument of soft power in Russian foreign policy. Public administration of the Russian federation: Challenges and prospects. In *Materials of the 15th international conference public administration in the XXI century* (pp. 558–563). Moscow: Moscow State University]. (In Russian).

The New Public Diplomacy: Soft Power in International Relations. (2005). J. Melissen (Ed.). Houndmills, Basingstoke, Hampshire: Palgrave Macmillan. Retrieved from www.culturaldiplomacy.org/academy/pdf/research/books/soft_power/The_New_Public_Diplomacy

Neymark, M. A. (2016). "Myagkaya sila" v mirovoy politike. K utochneniyu problemnogo polya (chast' 1). *Obozrevatel'/Observer, 1*(312), 31–42 [Neimark, M. A. (2016). Soft power in world politics. To clarify the problem field (part 1). *Observer, 1*(312), 31–42]. (In Russian).

Neymark, M. A. (2017). *"Myagkaya sila" v mirovoy politike*. Moskva: Dashkov i K° [Neimark, M. A. (2017). *Soft power in world politics*. Moscow: Dashkov and K°]. (In Russian).

Nikitina, Yu A. (2017). Publichnaya diplomatiya v rabote mezhpravitel'stvennykh organizatsiy na primere ODKB i SHOS. In M. M. Lebedeva (red.), *Publichnaya diplomatiya: Teoriya i praktika* (S. 112–127). Moskva: Aspekt Press [Nikitina, Yu A. (2017). Public diplomacy in the work of intergovernmental organizations on the example of the CSTO and SCO. In M. M. Lebedeva (Ed.), *Public diplomacy: Theory and practice* (pp. 112–127). Moscow: Aspect Press]. (In Russian).

Nye J. 2002. *The Paradox of American Power: Why the World's Only Superpower Can't Go it Alone*. New York: Oxford University Press.

Nye, J. S. (1990). *Bound to lead: The changing nature of American power*. New York: Basic Books.

Nye, J. S. (2004a). Soft power and higher education. *EDUCAUSE*. Retrieved from https://cdn.mashreghnews.ir/old/files/fa/news/1393/4/11/637473_515.pdf

Nye, J. S. (2004b). *Soft power. The means to success in world politics*. New York: Public Affairs.

Nye, J. S. (2008). Public diplomacy and soft power. *Annals of the American Academy of Political and Social Science, 16*(1), 94–109. doi:10.1177/0002716207311699

Nye, J. S. (2018, January 5). China's soft and sharp power. *China-US Focus*. Retrieved from www.chinausfocus.com/society-culture/chinas-soft-and-sharp-power-

Orlova, V. V. (2003). *Global'nyye teleseti novostey na informatsionnom rynke*. Seriya "Prakticheskaya zhurnalistika". Moskva: Izdatel'stvo "RIP-kholding". Retrieved from http://evartist.narod.ru/text5/68.htm [Orlova, V. V. (2003). *Global news networks in the information market*. "Practical Journalism Series". Moscow: Publishing house "RIP-holding". Retrieved from http://evartist.narod.ru/text5/68.htm]. (In Russian).

Ovchinnikova, N., Zotkina, M., & Getmanskaya, A. (2019). *Gosudarstvennyye programmy obrazovatel'noy mobil'nosti v raznykh stranakh*. Moskva: Tsentr transformatsii obrazovaniya Moskovskoy shkoly upravleniya SKOLKOVO. Retrieved from https://skolkovo.ru/public/media/documents/research/sedec/SKOLKOVO_SEDeC_International_Mobility_2019.pdf [Ovchinnikova, N., Zotkina, M., & Getmanskaya, A. (2019). *State educational mobility programs in different countries*. Moscow: Education Transformation Center of the Moscow School of Management SKOLKOVO. Retrieved from https://skolkovo.ru/public/

References

media/documents/research/sedec/SKOLKOVO_SEDeC_International_Mobility_2019.pdf]. (In Russian).

Panarin, I. N. (2016). Gladiatory gibridnoy voyny. *Ekonomicheskiye strategii, 18*(2), 60–65 [Panarin, I. N. (2016). Gladiators of the hybrid war. *Economic Strategies, 18*(2), 60–65]. (In Russian).

Panova, Ye P. (2010). Sila privlekatel'nosti: ispol'zovaniye "myagkoy sily" v mirovoy politike. *Vestnik MGIMO-Universiteta, 4*, 91–97 [Panova, E. P. (2010). The power of attractiveness: The use of soft power in world politics. *MGIMO Review of International Relations, 4*, 91–97 (In Russian).

Panova, Ye P. (2011). Vyssheye obrazovaniye kak instrument myagkoy vlasti gosudarstva. *Vestnik MGIMO – Universiteta, 2*(15), 157–161 [Panova, E. P. (2011). Higher education as an instrument of soft power of the state. *MGIMO Review of International Relations, 2*(15), 157–161]. (In Russian).

Panova, Ye P. (2012). *"Myagkaya vlast'" kak sposob vozdeystviya v mirovoy politike*. Dissertatsiya na stepen' kand. polit. n. Moskva: MGIMO (Universitet) [Panova, E. P. (2012). *The soft power as a way to influence in world politics* (PhD thesis). Moscow: MGIMO (University)]. (In Russian).

Parshin, P. B. (2014). Dva ponimaniya "myagkoy sily": Predposylki, korrelyaty i sledstviya. *Vestnik MGIMO Universiteta, 2*(35), 14–21. Retrieved from http://vestnik.mgimo.ru/sites/default/files/pdf/parshin.pdf [Parshin, P. B. (2014). Two understandings of soft power: Backgrounds, correlates, and effects. *MGIMO Review of International Relations, 2*(35), 14–21. Retrieved from http://vestnik.mgimo.ru/sites/default/files/pdf/parshin.pdf]. (In Russian).

Parubochnaya, Ye F., & Piskunov, N. V. (2018). Obshchestvennaya diplomatiya kak instrument realizatsii rossiyskoy "myagkoy sily". *Vestnik Volgogradskogo gosudarstvennogo universiteta. Seriya 4. Istoriya. Regionovedeniye. Mezhdunarodnyye otnosheniya, 23*(6), 197–207 [Parubochnaya, E. F., & Piskunov, N. V. (2018). Public diplomacy as a tool for implementing Russian soft power. *Bulletin of the Volgograd State University. Series 4. History. Regional Studies. International Relationships, 23*(6), 197–207]. (In Russian).

Permyakova, L. (2012). Tsifrovaya diplomatiya: napravleniya raboty, riski i instrumenty. Sentyabr' 27. Sayt RSMD. Retrieved from http://russiancouncil.ru/inner/?id_4=862#top [Permyakova, L. (2012). Digital diplomacy: directions of work, risks and tools. September 27. RIAC website. Retrieved from http://russiancouncil.ru/inner/?id_4=862#top (In Russian).

Permyakova, L., & Skryagina, S. (2013). Sotsial'naya otvetstvennost' kak "myagkaya sila" transnatsional'nykh kompaniy. *Diplomaticheskaya sluzhba, 4*, 76–80 [Permyakova, L., & Skryagina, S. (2013). Social responsibility as soft power of transnational companies. *Diplomatic Service, 4*, 76–80]. (In Russian).

Pestsov, S. K., & Bobylo, A. M. (2015). "Myagkaya sila" v mirovoy politike: problema operatsionalizatsii teoreticheskogo kontsepta. *Vestnik Tomskogo gosudarstvennogo universiteta. Istoriya, 2*(34), 108–114 [Pestsov, S. K., & Bobylo, A. M. (2015). Soft power in world politics: The problem of operationalization of a theoretical concept. *Bulletin of Tomsk State University. History, 2*(34), 108–114]. (In Russian).

Podberezkin, A. I. (2016). Voyennaya sila i politika novoy publichnoy diplomatii. *Obozrevatel'*, *12*(323), 15–25 [Podberezkin, A. (2016). Military force and the policy of new public diplomacy. *Reviewer*, *12*(323), 15–25]. (In Russian).

Podberezkin, A. I., & Zhukov, A. V. (2015). Publichnaya diplomatiya v silovom protivostoyanii tsivilizatsiy. *Vestnik MGIMO-Universiteta*, *6*(45), 106–116 [Podberezkin, A. I., & Zhukov, A. V. (2015). Public diplomacy in the violent confrontation of civilizations. *MGIMO Review of International Relations*, *6*(45), 106–116]. (In Russian).

Routledge Handbook of Public Diplomacy. (2008). Snow, N., & Taylor, Ph M. (Eds.). New York: Routledge.

Rustamova, L. R. (2016). Osobennosti "myagkoy sily" vo vneshney politike FRG. *Vestnik MGIMO-Universitet*, *1*, 118–128 [Rustamova, L. R. (2016). Features of soft power in the foreign policy of Germany. *MGIMO Review of International Relations*, *1*, 118–128]. (In Russian).

Ryzhov, Yu A., & Lebedev, M. L. (2007). Yubiley Paguoshskogo dvizheniya. *Vestnik Rossiyskoy Akademii nauk*, *10*, 938–948 [Ryzhov, Yu A., & Lebedev, M. L. (2007). Anniversary of the Pugwash movement. *Bulletin of the Russian Academy of Sciences*, *10*, 938–948]. (In Russian).

Sedunov, A. V. (2017). Kul'turnaya diplomatiya kak instrument publichnoy diplomatii v Zabaykal'skom kraye RF. *Nauchnyy al'manakh*, *1*(35), 189–192. Retrieved from http://ucom.ru/doc/na.2017.09.01.189.pdf [Sedunov, A. V. (2017). Cultural diplomacy as an instrument of public diplomacy in the Trans-Baikal territory of the Russian federation. *Scientific Almanac*, *1*(35), 189–192. Retrieved from http://ucom.ru/doc/na.2017.09.01.01.189.pdf]. (In Russian).

Semedov, S. A., & Kurbatova, A. G. (2020). Russian public diplomacy and nation branding. In A. Velikaya & G. Simons (Eds.), *Russia's public diplomacy: Evolution and practice* (pp. 45–59). Palgrave Macmillan.

Shelepov, A. V. (2014). Zarubezhnyy opyt primeneniya "myagkoy sily". Faktory uspekha politiki "myagkoy sily" Velikobritanii. *Vestnik mezhdunarodnykh organizatsiy*, *9*(2), 10–25 [Shelepov, A. V. (2014). Foreign experience in the use of soft power. UK success factors for soft power policy. *International Organisations Research Journal*, *9*(2), 10–25]. (In Russian).

Shestopal, A. V., & Litvak, N. V. (2016). Nauchnaya diplomatiya. Opyt sovremennoy Frantsii. *Vestnik MGIMO-Universiteta*, *5*(50), 106–114 [Shestopal, A. V., & Litvak, N. V. (2016). Scientific diplomacy. The experience of modern France. *MGIMO Review of International Relations*, *5*(50), 106–114]. (In Russian)].

Shikhova, M. S. (2019). Primeneniye publichnoy diplomatii malymi gosudarstvami na primere Norvegii. In *Sbornik statey po materialam XXX mezhdunarodnoy nauchno-prakticheskoy konferentsii* (S. 30–40). Moskva: Obshchestvo s ogranichennoy otvetstvennost'yu "Mezhdunarodnyy tsentr nauki i obrazovaniya" [Shikhova, M. S. (2019). The use of public diplomacy by small states. Example of Norway. In *Materials of the XXX international scientific-practical conference* (pp. 30–40). Moscow: International Center for Science and Education]. (In Russian).

Shlapeko, Ye A. (2017). Institut obshchestvennoy diplomatii i yego mesto v transgranichnom sotsiokul'turnom prostranstve. *Oykumena*, *1*, 152–162. Retrieved from https://ojkum.ru/images/articles/2019-1/_2019_1_17-25.pdf [Shlapeko, E. A. (2017). Institute for public diplomacy and its place in a transboundary sociocultural space. *Oikumena*, *1*, 152–162. Retrieved from https://ojkum.ru/images/articles/2019-1/_2019_1_17-25.pdf].

Simons, G. (2014). Russian public diplomacy in the 21st century: Structure, means and message. *Public Relations Review*, *40*(3), 440–449. doi:10.1016/j.pubrev.2014.03.002.

Snow, N. (2010). Public diplomacy: New dimensions and implications. In T. L. McPhail (Ed.), *Global communication: Theories, stakeholders and trends* (3rd ed., pp. 84–102). Chichester: Wiley-Blackwell.

Soft power: teoriya, resursy, diskurs. (2014). O. F. Rusakova (red.). Yekaterinburg: Izdatel'skiy dom "Diskurs-Pi" [*Soft power: Theory, resourses, discource*. (2014). O. F. Rusakova (Ed.). Yekaterinburg: Publishing House "Diskurs-Pi"].

Sovetskaya kul'turnaya diplomatiya v usloviyakh Kholodnoy voyny (1945–1989). (2018). O. S. Nagornaya (Ed.). Moskva: Politicheskaya Entsiklopediya [*Soviet Cultural Diplomacy During the Cold War (1945–1989)*. (2018). O. S. Nagornaya (Ed.). Moscow: Political Encyclopedia]. (In Russian).

Stetsko, E. (2020). The role of civil society in Russian public diplomacy. Russian public diplomacy and nation branding. In A. Velikaya & G. Simons (Eds.), *Russia's public diplomacy: Evolution and practice* (pp. 147–166). Palgrave Macmillan.

Sveshnikov, A. A. (2001). Kontseptsii KNR v oblasti vneshney politiki i natsional'noy bezopasnosti. In *Kitay v mirovoy politike* (S. 93–143). Moskva: ROSSPEN [Sveshnikov, A. A. (2001). PRC concepts in the field of foreign policy and national security. In *China in world politics* (pp. 93–143). Moscow: ROSSPEN]. (In Russian).

Tabarintseva-Romanova, K. M. (2019). "Novyye" vidy diplomatii XXI v.: kul'turnaya diplomatiya v sovremennom mezhdunarodnom diskurse. *Nauchnyy zhurnal "Diskurs-Pi"*, *3*(36), 26–37. https://cyberleninka.ru/article/n/novye-vidy-diplomatii-xxi-v-kulturnaya-diplomatiya-v-sovremennom-mezhdunarodnom-diskurse/viewer [Tabarintseva-Romanova, K. M. (2019). "New" types of diplomacy of the XXI century: Cultural diplomacy in modern international discourse. *Scientific Journal "Discourse-Pi"*, *3*(36), 26–37. https://cyberleninka.ru/article/n/novye-vidy-diplomatii-xxi-v-kulturnaya-diplomatiya-v-sovremennom-mezhdunarodnom-diskurse/viewer]. (In Russian).

Tabarintseva-Romanova, K. M. (2020, maya 8). Borshch, vino i tropicheskiy ray. *Rossiyskiy Sovet po mezhdunarodnym delam*. Retrieved from https://russiancouncil.ru/analytics-and-comments/columns/otherside/borshch-vino-i-tropicheskiy-ray/?sphrase_id=36796086 [Tabarintseva-Romanova, K. (2020, May 8). Borsch, wine and tropical paradise. *Russian Council on Foreign Affairs*. Retrieved from https://russiancouncil.ru/analytics-and-comments/columns/otherside/borshch-vino-i-tropicheskiy-ray/?sphrase_id=36796086]. (In Russian).

Tandoc, E. C., Jr., Zheng, W. L., & Ling, R. (2017, September). Defining "fake news". A typology of scholarly definitions. *Digital Journalism*, 1–17. Retrieved from www.researchgate.net/publication/319383049_Defining_Fake_News_A_typology_of_scholarly_definitions

References

Tkachenko, S. (2020). Development diplomacy of the Russian federation. Russian public diplomacy and nation branding. In A. Velikaya & G. Simons (Eds.), *Russia's public diplomacy: Evolution and practice* (pp. 61–77). Palgrave Macmillan.

Torkunov, A. V. (2012). Obrazovaniye kak instrument "myagkoy sily" vo vneshney politike Rossii. *Vestnik MGIMO – Universitet. Vestnik MGIMO – Universiteta, 4*(25), 85–93 [Torkunov, A. V. (2012). Education as an instrument of soft power in Russian foreign policy. *MGIMO Review of International Relations, 4*(25), 85–93]. (In Russian).

Torkunov, A. V. (2019). Diplomatiya akademicheskogo soobshchestva: proshloye i nastoyashcheye. *Mirovaya ekonomika i mezhdunarodnyye otnosheniya, 63*(9), 22–28. https://doi.org/10.20542/0131-2227-2019-63-9-22-28 [Torkunov, A. (2019). Diplomacy of the academic community: Past and present. *World Economy and International Relations, 63*(9), 22–28. https://doi.org/10.20542/0131-2227-2019-63-9-22-22-28]. (In Russian).

Tsvetkova, N. A. (2011). Programmy Web 2.0 v publichnoy diplomatii SShA. *SShA i Kanada: Ekonomika, politika, kul'tura, 3*, 109–122 [Tsvetkova, N. (2011). Web 2.0 programs in US public diplomacy. *USA and Canada: Economics, Politics, Culture, 3*, 109–122]. (In Russian).

Tsvetkova, N. A. (2012). Publichnaya diplomatiya SShA v Rossii: ot "demokratizatsii" k razvitiyu "sotsial'nogo aktivizma". *SShA i Kanada: ekonomika, politika, kul'tura, 10*(514), 37–46 [Tsvetkova, N. A. (2012). US public diplomacy in Russia: From "democratization" to the development of "social activism". *USA and Canada: Economics, Politics, Culture, 10*(514), 37–46]. (In Russian).

Tsvetkova, N. A. (2015). Publichnaya diplomatiya SSHA ot "myagkoy sily" k dialogovoy propagande. *Mezhdunarodnyye protsessy, 13*(3), 121–133. doi:10.17994/IT.2015.13.2.42.8. Retrieved from http://intertrends.ru/system/Doc/ArticlePdf/1248/A7xHW3zLY9.pdf [Tsvetkova, N. (2015). Public diplomacy of the USA from soft power to dialogue propaganda. *International Processes, 13*(3), 121–133. doi:10.17994/IT.2015.13.2.4.4.8. Retrieved from http://intertrends.ru/system/Doc/ArticlePdf/1248/A7xHW3zLY9.pdf]. (In Russian).

Tsvetkova, N. A. (2020). Russian digital diplomacy: A rising cyber soft power? In A. Velikaya & G. Simons (Eds.), *Russia's public diplomacy: Evolution and practice* (pp. 103–117). Palgrave Macmillan.

Tsygankov, A. (2006). If not by tanks, then by banks? The role of soft power in Putin's foreign policy. *Europe-Asia Studies, 58*(7), 1079–1099.

Vapler, V. Ya, Gronskaya, N. E., Gusev, A. S., Korshunov, D. S., Makarychev, A. S., & Solntsev, A. V. (2010). Ideya imperii i "myagkaya sila": mirovoy opyt i rossiyskiye perspektivy. *Voprosy upravleniya, 1*(10), 22–27. Retrieved from http://vestnik.uapa.ru/ru/issue/2010/01/02/ [Vapler, V. Ya, Gronskaya, N. E., Gusev, A. S., Korshunov, D. S., Makarychev, A. S., & Solntsev, A. V. (2010). The idea of empire and soft power: World experience and Russian prospects. *Management Issues, 1*(10), 22–27. Retrieved from http://vestnik.uapa.ru/ru/issue/2010/01/02/]. (In Russian).

Velikaya, A. A. (2019). Publichnaya diplomatiya Rossii i SShA: sravnitel'nyye aspekty dvukh sistem i rol' v razvitii dvustoronnego dialoga. *Vestnik Sankt-Peterburgskogo universiteta. Mezhdunarodnyye otnosheniya, 12*(4), 500–517. https://doi.org/10.21638/11701/spbu06.2019.407 [Great, A. A. (2019). Public diplomacy of Russia and the United States: Comparative aspects of the two systems and the role in the development of bilateral dialogue. *Bulletin of St. Petersburg University. International Relations*, *12*(4), 500–517. https://doi.org/10.21638/11701/spbu06.2019.407]. (In Russian).

Walker, C., & Ludwig, J. (2017, November 16). The meaning of sharp power – how authoritarian states project influence. *Foreign Affairs*, Retrieved from www.foreignaffairs.com/articles/china/2017-11-16/meaning-sharp-power?cid=int-fls&pgtype=hpg/

Yevdokimov, Ye V. (2011). "Narodnaya diplomatiya" KNR. Massovost' kak fenomen kitayskoy vneshnepoliticheskoy propagandy. *Vestnik MGIMO-universiteta*, *3*, 285–289 [Evdokimov, E. V. (2011). "People's diplomacy" of the PRC. Mass as a phenomenon of Chinese foreign policy propaganda. *MGIMO Review of International Relations*, *3*, 285–289]. (In Russian).

Zaharna, R. S. (2004). From propaganda to public diplomacy in the information age. In R. K. Yahya & S. Nancy (Eds.), *War, media, and propaganda: A global perspective* (pp. 219–226). Lanham, MD: Rowman and Littlefield.

Zaharna, R. S. (2007). The soft power differential: Network communication and mass communication in public diplomacy. *Hague Journal of Public Diplomacy*, *2*, 213–228.

Zegonov, O. V. (2008). Gosudarstva i SMI v kontekste miropoliticheskogo vzaimodeystviya. *Kosmopolis*, *1*(20), 51–65 [Zegonov, O. V. (2008). States and mass media in the context of world political interaction. *Cosmopolis*, *1*(20), 51–65]. (In Russian).

Zevelev, I. A., & Troitskiy, M. A. (2006). Sila i vliyaniye v amerikano-rossiyskikh otnosheniyakh: semioticheskiy analiz. *Ocherki tekushchey politiki. Vypusk 2*. Moskva: Nauchno-obrazovatel'nyy forum po mezhdunarodnym otnosheniyam [Zevelev, I. A., & Troitsky, M. A. (2006). Strength and influence in US-Russian relations: A semiotic analysis. In *Essays on current politics. Issue 2*. Moscow: Scientific and Educational Forum on International Relations]. (In Russian).

Zinov'yeva, Ye S. (2016). Tsifrovaya diplomatiya, mezhdunarodnaya bezopasnost' i vozmozhnosti dlya Rossii. *Indeks bezopasnosti*, *1*(104), 213–228 [Zinov'yeva, E. (2016). Digital diplomacy, international security and opportunities for Russia. *Safety Index*, *1*(104), 213–228]. (In Russian).

Zinov'yeva, Ye S. (2017). Tsifrovaya publichnaya diplomatiya kak instrument uregulirovaniya konfliktov. In M. M. Lebedeva (red.), *Publichnaya diplomatiya: Teoriya i praktika* (S. 54–69). Moskva: Aspekt Press [Zinov'yeva, E. S. (2017). Digital public diplomacy as a tool for conflict resolution. In M. M. Lebedeva (Ed.), *Public diplomacy: Theory and practice* (pp. 54–69). Moscow: Aspect Press]. (In Russian).

Zonova, T. V. (2004). Diplomatiya kak instrument kul'tury mira i tolerantnosti. In *Kul'tura tolerantnosti: opyt diplomatii dlya resheniya sovremennykh upravlencheskikh problem* (S. 215–241). Moskva: MGIMO [Zonova, T. (2004). Diplomacy as an instrument of the culture of peace and tolerance. In *A culture of tolerance: The experience of diplomacy for solving modern management problems* (pp. 215–241). Moscow: MGIMO]. (In Russian).

Zonova, T. V. (2012). Publichnaya diplomatiya i yeyo aktory. *Rossiyskiy sovet po mezhdunarodnym delam*. Retrieved from http://russiancouncil.ru/analytics-and-comments/analytics/publichnaya-diplomatiya-i-ee-aktory/ [Zonova, T. (2012). Public diplomacy and its actors. *Russian Council on Foreign Affairs*. Retrieved from http://russiancouncil.ru/analytics-and-comments/analytics/publichnaya-diplo matiya-i-ee-aktory/]. (In Russian).

Zonova, T. V. (2017). Publichnaya diplomatiya Yevropeyskogo soyuza. In M. M. Lebedeva (red.), *Publichnaya diplomatiya: Teoriya i praktika* (S. 70–88). Moskva: Aspekt Press [Zonova, T. V. (2017). Public diplomacy of the European Union. In M. M. Lebedeva (Ed.), *Public diplomacy: Theory and practice* (pp. 70–88). Moscow: Aspect Press]. (In Russian).

Zubkova, A. (2015). Myagkaya sila Turtsii: Fenomen "Soap Power" kak instrumenta kul'turnoy diplomatii. *Vestnik RUDN. Seriya Politologiya*, *2*, 52–62 [Zubkova, A. (2015). The soft power of Turkey: The phenomenon of "soap power" as an instrument of cultural diplomacy. *Bulletin of the RUDN University. Series Political Science*, *2*, 52–62]. (In Russian).

Index

Note: Page numbers in **bold** indicate a table on the corresponding page.

academic diplomacy 46
academic exchanges 22
academic literature 20, 28, 31, 33–34, 47
Afghanistan, Russian troops in 16
Africa 23, 39
Alexander Gorchakov Public Diplomacy Fund, The 21
Alliance Française 15
All-Union Society for Cultural Relations with Foreign Countries (VOKS) 14–15; *see also* culture
American dominance 38
Argentina 21
Armenia 40
Asia 23
attitude 34
attracting-engaging 36–37
attractiveness: creation of 6, 12, 47; of educational services 45; initiation of 14; propaganda and 6–7; of Russia and Belarus 42; of Russian education 45; soft power and 5, 10, 28–29, 37, 47
authoritarian regimes 8

Balkan, Baltic, and Caucasian Dialogues 21
Baltic countries 23, 36
BBC 15
Belarus 42
Belgium 33
beliefs and public diplomacy 6
blackmail 7
Bologna Process 23
boycott of Olympic Games 15–16

Brazil 21, 33
BRICS 23–24
British public diplomacy 38
broadcasting 15, 21
business: diplomacy 31; relations 38; structures 31

Central Asia 35, 39
centralization 34
Children's Musical Theater of the Young Actor (DMTUA) 24
China 35, 38–39
cinema, use in public diplomacy 40
CIS states 23–24, 35, 45
citizens: abroad, contact with 43; diplomacy 29
civil societies: institutions 18–19; NGOs and active 33; potential and foreign policy 19; representatives 21; of Russia and France 24, 30, 33; of Russia and internal Russian dialogue 30
close ties 30
coercion 28
Cold War 9, 11, 15, 36, 45
Collective Security Treaty Organization (CSTO) 41
commercial agreements 31
Commonwealth of Independent States 20
communication, modern means of 16
compatriots 20, 22, 32, 33, 42, 47
competition 29
"Concept of export of educational services of the Russian Federation for the period 2011–2020" 23

conflict resolution 41, 44, 45
Confucius centers 39
constructive dialogue 36
constructivist approach 28–29
consular activities 43
cooperation 28, 31, 38
coordination 34, 35
creative diplomacy 22
criticism 32
culinary diplomacy 36
cultural cooperation 20, 34, 38
cultural diplomacy of Iran 40
cultural diplomacy of Russia: activities 24, 35; need for 18; overview 16; regional aspects of 44; as representative of public diplomacy 32, 33; Russian studies on 47
cultural heritage 39
cultural identity 19
culture: Chinese 38–39; of foreign states 15; promotion in Iran 39; soft power and 38–39; of United States 36–37; *see also* VOKS (All-Union Society for Cultural Relations with Foreign Countries)
culture, Russian: achievements of 18; centers of 20; education and 23; promotion 37–38, 45; research on role of 44; Russian language and 21–22, 35, 37; *see also* VOKS (All-Union Society for Cultural Relations with Foreign Countries)
cyber propaganda 43; *see also* propaganda

Daily Telegraph, The 21
Dartmouth Conferences 15
democracy, universal values of 37
desire 28
developing countries 22
development diplomacy 31
dialogue: between Iran and Central Asian states 39; between societies 32; constructive 36; cultural diplomacy and 47; education and 23; EU, achieving goals through 41; as feature of public diplomacy 5, 8; with foreign audiences 6, 12; internal Russian dialogue 30; of mutual understanding and cooperation 28; need for 30; by Russian Orthodox Church 24; Trianon Dialogue 24

Dialogue for the Future 21
digital diplomacy 42–44
diplomatic discourse 36
domestic issues 36
domination (*vlast*), soft power as 28
donations 38

Eastern Europe 38
economic coercion 28
economic cooperation 31, 37
economic (or business) diplomacy 31
e-diplomacy 42
education 22, 23, 35, 38, 45–46; diplomacy 46; exchange programs 35; programs 44
English-language service 15
environmental issues 35
Estonia 14
ethnic strife 24
EU (European Union) 5, 24, 37, 41
Eurasian Economic Union (EAEU) 40, 41
Europe 23
European Commission 41
European countries 23, 38–39
exchange programs 41
exhibition activities 24
external audience, influencing 12

Facebook diplomacy 32
fake news 2, 6, 11–12
federal budgets 38
feedback 35
FIFA World Cup 22
Figaro, Le 21
Fletcher School of Law and Diplomacy 3, 6
flexible power (*gibkaya sila*), soft power as 28
foreign audiences: dialogue with 6; influencing 5, 11–12, 18–20, 24, 42–44; interaction with 15–16, 40
foreign broadcasting channels 20–21
foreign citizens, educational services to 45
foreign governments 30
Foreign Ministry's Center for Public and Media Diplomacy 39–40
foreign NGOs 15; *see also* NGOs
foreign policy: activation in Russia 17–18; concepts of the Russian Federation 18–19; goals 31

foreign PR agencies 24
foreign society, representatives of 11
foreign students 23
France 24, 33, 37
funding 21, 23, 32, 35, 38–39

G2P (government to people) interaction 5, 16
G8 summit 24
Genoese Conference 14
Georgia 23, 40
Germany 37–38
global competition 19, 23
Gorchakov Fund 22
Great Britain 37

heterogeneous society 10
higher education 23, 45–46
historical heritage 39
history, falsification of 32–33
humanitarian cooperation 20, 33, 34, 38
humanitarian resources 1–2, 5
human rights 19, 35
hybrid wars 2, 43

ideological dialogue 24
image creation 32, 41
incentives (rewards) **8**
incomes 38
India 21
influence 9, 28, 47; *see also* foreign audiences, influencing
informal communication channels 36
information: analysis 42–43; and communication technologies 5, 19, 24, 34, 44; wars 9, 10, 43, 47
informational influence 18, 43
innovative cooperation 38
interference 29, 36
intergovernmental organizations 41
international contacts 24
international cooperation 20, 30
international development 37
internationalization of education 23
international organizations 5, 33, 40–41
international public space 32
international recognition of Russia 14
international relations 1, 10–11, 21–22, 30, 46
international sports competitions 22
international youth cooperation 32

Internet 37, 42, 43, 46
Iran 38–39, 40
Irkutsk 24
Islamic revolution 39–40
Italy 21, 36

Justice and Development Party 40

Karelia, Republic of 44
Kazakhstan 40
Ketchum 24

language, Chinese 39
language, Russian: barrier 23; diplomacy 32; interaction with compatriots 20; media 19; promotion 21–22, 37, 38, 45; spread of 41
Latin America 23, 38, 39
Latvia, Republic of 14
literature, Russian 22
Lithuania 36
lobbying 29
long-term interaction **8**

"Main Directions of Russian Policy in the Field of International Cultural and Humanitarian Cooperation, The" 18
manipulation 6–7, **8**
mass audience 46–47
mass communication 46
mass media 20–21, 36
media 15, 19, 36, 46–47
medical assistance 33
medicine and science 35
membership fees 38
Middle East 4, 37, 40
migrants 32
military, hierarchy of relations in 9–10
military-political resources 2
mobility programs 23
modern world politics 36
monologue **8**
Moscow Radio 15
multilingual channels 40
multinational corporations 31
Muslim countries, Turkic-speaking 40
mutual understanding 28, 30, 32

national branding 2, 10–11, 30–31
national values 38

NATO 9, 36
neoliberalism 7, **8**, 28–29
neo-Ottomanism 40
network-centric hybrid warfare 43
network universities 23–24
newspaper materials 21
NGOs: activities of 29–30; diplomacy of 22, 30; foreign, in Russia 15; German 38; Russian, peculiarities of 34; state-supported 32; working in UN and 33
Nizhny Novgorod 24
non-state actors: as "conductors" 9, 11; funding of 38; increase in 4–5, 18–19; role of 18; state's action through 29–32
non-state structures-conductors 9
Norway 40
Nye's concept of soft power: public diplomacy and 2, 5, 6–8; public diplomacy in Russia and 27–28, 31, 36; Russian objection on 17–18

Obama administration 37, 43
official media channels 36
official representatives 29
Olympic Games 15–16
openness 5, 6, 12

parliamentary diplomacy 32, 42, 47
partner university 23–24
peacemaking 16
people's diplomacy 29–30; *see also* public diplomacy
Peoples' Friendship University 22–23
Persian culture 39
policy-making 29
political coercion 28
political discourse 36
political-economic resources 2
political forecasts 42–43
political institutions 36
portal 24
pressure 7
Primakov Readings 46
Prologue Children's Theater Festival 24
propaganda: communist 4; cyber 43–44; difference from soft power 29; media and 47; public diplomacy and 5–12, 32; US public diplomacy and 37

public diplomacy: in 1990s and early 2000s 16–18; characteristics of 11–13; definitions of 3–4, 37; development of appropriate structures 20–24; national branding and 10–11; origins 14–16; propaganda and 5–12, 32; revival of 4–5; sharp power and 8; and soft power in foreign policy concepts 18–19; strategic communication and 8–10; supranational 5
public diplomacy in 2000s: other areas of public diplomacy 42–47; theoretical research 27–32; of various states and international organizations 32–42
public opinion 7, 17, 19, 21
public policy 31
public speeches 14
Pugwash movement 15

radio broadcasting 21
Radio Moscow World Service 15, 17
realism 6–7, **8**, 17, 29
regional budgets 38
religious diplomacy 42, 47
religious resource 39
RIA Novosti news agency 20, 21
rivalry 29
Rossiya Segodnya 21
Rossiyskaya Gazeta 21
Rossotrudnichestvo 20, 33, 40
Roszarubezhtsentr 20
Russian Association for International Cooperation (RAMS) 16–17
Russian Center for International Scientific and Cultural Cooperation 16
Russian dialogue, internal 30
Russian Foreign Policy Concept 18–19
Russian foreign policy vocabulary 30; *see also* language, Russian
Russian Humanitarian Mission 40
Russian-language media 19; *see also* mass media; media
Russian Orthodox Church (ROC) 24, 40
Russian Peoples' Friendship University (RUDN) 22–23
Russian troops in Afghanistan 16
Russian universities 22

Russia Today (RT) 20–21, 46
Russkiy Mir Foundation 21–22

scholars: American 4; Russian 15, 16, 27, 29, 30, 38, 39, 42
science: conferences 39; cooperation 38; diplomacy 16, 45–46; discourse 28; and education 37; literature, Russian 43; ties 15
scientists 15, 24
SCO 23–24
self-tuning 35
semi-state structures-conductors 9
smart power 6
Sochi Olympic Games 22
social group 10
social networks 5, 20, 24, 40, 42, 46
social resources 1–2, 5
social responsibility 31
soft power: concept of 6; EU's 41; in the foreign policy concepts of the Russian Federation 18–19; hard power *versus* 7–8; interpretations of 27–29; policy of Great Britain 38; politics, fallout in Turkey 40; public diplomacy and 2, 5, 6–8; public diplomacy in Russia and 27–28, 31, 36; *see also* Nye's concept of soft power
South Caucasus 40
Soviet Cultural Diplomacy in the Cold War (1945–1989) (Nagornaya) 16
Soviet scientists 15
Soviet Union 9
sports: diplomacy 15–16, 22, 44; and tourism 35
Sputnik Agency 21
state and society 5
state funding 38; *see also* funding
state-supported NGOs 32; *see also* NGOs
St. Petersburg 24
St. Petersburg University 36
strategic communication: concept of 8–9; influencing external audience through 12; North Atlantic Treaty Organization (NATO) and 9; popularity of 10, 43; Russian public diplomacy and 43–44, 47; in the US 37
strategic planning 43
student exchange programs 23

supranational associations 42
supranational public diplomacy 5
supranational structures 35, 40–41
suspicion 10

Tajikistan 39
technical cooperation 38
terrorist attacks of 9/11 4
tourism 11, 24, 39
trainings 23, 34
Trianon Dialogue 24
trust **8**, 10, 15
Turkey, public diplomacy 40
twinning ties 33
Twitter diplomacy 32, 42

UN 5, 24, 33
UN Economic and Social Council (ECOSOC) 33
UNESCO 23
UNESCO World Heritage List 39
Union of Soviet Societies for Friendship and Cultural Relations with Foreign Countries (SSOD) 15
unions 5
universal values of democracy 37
Universiade in Kazan 22
US: culture of 36–37; digital diplomacy 37, 43; foreign policy 36; sanctions 28

Valdai Discussion Club, international 46
Vladivostok 24
Voice of America 15
Voice of Russia radio 16–17, 20, 21
VOKS (All-Union Society for Cultural Relations with Foreign Countries) 14–15; *see also* culture

Walker, C. 8
Washington Post 21
water diplomacy 39
Web 2.0 diplomacy 42
websites 20, 42
Western countries 8
Western European international cooperation 30
world politics 36, 42

Yekaterinburg 24, 29
youth: contacts 42; diplomacy 35, 47

For Product Safety Concerns and Information please contact our EU representative GPSR@taylorandfrancis.com
Taylor & Francis Verlag GmbH, Kaufingerstraße 24, 80331 München, Germany

www.ingramcontent.com/pod-product-compliance
Lightning Source LLC
Chambersburg PA
CBHW070602170426
43201CB00012B/1908